Dear Lee,

I just finished reading I *Loved* Lucy. Bravo. Congratulations! I couldn't put it down. And I couldn't *wait* to tell you so. What a refreshing piece of entertainment and what a wonderful "look through the keyhole" at this very unique and complicated woman. I don't know how you were able to capture her so accurately. But what a great, fun, compassionate realization of who this legend *really* was, and a more perfect portrait of the "lost Lucy years" I cannot imagine being drawn . . . even by me. It had me in tears. Good tears.

I am very impressed. And I am extremely grateful to you for the graceful way you found to tell some very hard truths. It's time. I know you said you wrote it for you and yet it will help many, many people (including me) to know Lucy and understand her better, deeper. And, fear not, we will love her even more because, like us, she was only human.

People should read this.

Much love,

Lucie Arnaz

Lee —

Ours is a

really valuable

friendship to me —

Love

Lucy

LEE TANNEN

I ♡ Loved Lucy

My Friendship with Lucille Ball

 ST MARTIN'S GRIFFIN ⚏ NEW YORK

www.stmartins.com

Design by Sue Walsh

Library of Congress Cataloging-in-Publication Data

Tannen, Lee.
    I loved Lucy : my friendship with Lucille Ball / Lee Tannen.
        p. cm.
    ISBN 0-312-28753-4 (hc)
    ISBN 0-312-30274-6 (pbk)
    1. Ball, Lucille, 1911 2. Tannen, Lee. 3. Comedians—United States—Biography. 4. Entertainers—United States—Biography. I. Title.

PN2287.B16 T36 2001
791.45'028'092—dc21
[B]   2001041726

First St. Martin's Griffin Edition: October 2002

10   9   8   7   6   5   4   3   2   1

For JWW

Contents ✳

Contents

✳ *Acknowledgments* ✳

I don't know how all this happened. One very early morning about a year and a half ago I sat down at my laptop, which sits atop an otherwise unused backgammon table, and started to write my memories of Lucy. The next thing I knew, I've got a couple hundred pages and a terrific agent named Al Lowman at Authors and Artists who tells me he sold my memoir to a fabulous editor at St. Martin's Press named Elizabeth Beier.

Somewhere between page one and "Congratulations, it's a book!" there are others to thank for their encouragement, support, and love. Although it's all still a bit of a blur, let me clearly acknowledge those who helped make my dream come true: Tom Wells, Lucie Arnaz, Wanda Clark, David Zippel, Therese Steiner, Rick Moranis, Tom Watson, Frank Gorey, Susie Adamson, David Friddle, Mary Wells, Karen Burnes, Aunt Sylvia, Pat and Charlie Stone, Betty Ross, Fritz Friedman, PBS (the lady, not the network), Ric Wyman, Bob Policastro, Alix Nelson, Margo and Lucy Esmeralda.

I'm also grateful to a great bunch of people at St. Martin's Press, including Steve Snider, Michael Connor, John Murphy, John Karle, and Sara K. Delson.

What can I say about Phil Lobel and the staff of Lobeline Communications? Except to say that if you ever need anything publicized, promoted, pushed, prodded, or plugged, Phil is the guy to call. I can never thank him enough for loving "Lucy" so much!

A special thanks to the first Lucille in my life, my mother, who married my father Bob who had a first cousin named Bob who married a lady named Helen who had a brother named Gary who married a redhead named Lucy.

Author's Note ✳

I LOVED LUCY IS DRAWN SOLELY from memory—a remembrance of a friendship and of a time in my life spent with a remarkable woman named Lucille Ball at the end of hers. It's a loving and candid portrait of a woman of prodigious gifts and prodigious complexity. A valentine to my very own "Auntie Mame."

These reminiscences for the most part speak for themselves. At times I've tried to offer explanations as to why Lucy acted the way she acted—to me and to others close in her life. With Lucy, nothing was ever simple. So in looking back, more than a decade after her death, a lot of things about Lucy still perplex me and at times I still scratch my head looking for answers. It's one of the reasons I wrote this book. Maybe you'll read between the lines and understand things about Lucy I never did.

The one thing I do know is that I loved Lucy—I still do, and I'll never forget her. And in all the years I knew Lucy, no matter with whom I spoke about her, everybody asked, "What was she like? Was she *really* like Lucy Ricardo?" My knee-jerk response was always, "No way!" Now I'm not so sure. Both were clowns who would use laughs in order to get their own way. And, if they had to, just as easily tears. Both could be maddening one minute, irresistible the next. Both not only wanted to get into the act, they *needed* to be the star! The big difference between the alter egos was that the end of each Lucy episode *always* brought a happy ending. That was not always so in real life.

I am not one of Lucille Ball's biographers. Although we were almost forty years apart in age, we were the closest and dearest of friends. Most people who wrote about Lucy's life never *really* knew her; they relied on others who did to fill in the blanks. I relied on Lucy.

Desi Arnaz once said, "*I Love Lucy* was never just the title of a television show." *I Loved Lucy* is not just the title of a book.

—Lee Tannen
New York City, 2001

The Pilot Episode

I'VE WANTED TO WRITE THIS MEMOIR for a long time—since April 26, 1989, the day Lucy died. And every time I started, I stopped. "Who would want to read a book about my life with Lucy by somebody nobody ever heard of?" So I would tell my friends about Lucy and me and the glorious places we traveled to, and the wonderful things we did together, and the unforgettable stories she told me. In April 2000 Rex Reed called and said he was doing an oral history about the private life of Lucille Ball for *Talk* magazine. He had heard about my relationship with Lucy from Paula Stewart, Lucy's friend and costar of *Wildcat*, the only Broadway show Lucy ever did. He wanted to talk with me about the personal side of a very public woman I was extremely close to during the last decade of her life. I told Rex I was very apprehensive about doing so. Besides I really had nothing bad or salacious to say about Lucy. What kind of story would *that* make? He convinced me that *whatever* I had to say about her would be printed exactly as I told him.

We spoke on the phone for more than two hours and Rex taped memories of Lucy and me that poured out. When the *Talk* piece was published Rex had kept his promise and what I said was printed verbatim. I then kept the promise I made to myself over a decade ago to write a story about how much I loved Lucy.

So here goes.

Can you imagine walking up Third Avenue in Manhattan with Lucille Ball and ducking into P. J. Bernstein's, a delicatessen around the corner from where she lived, for franks and beans, one of her favorite meals, with no wig or makeup, just a rag around her head? Then the next week you're sitting next to Lucy at a State Department dinner in her honor and she's dressed to the nines feasting on roasted quail, one of her least favorite dishes? Can you imagine being together at *La Cage Aux Folles* on Broadway and she gets the biggest standing ovation for just sitting in the audience? Can you imagine sitting next to her when she's behind the wheel of her Mercedes tying up traffic for blocks trying to parallel park on Rodeo Drive? Or nearly getting arrested for merely being locked out of her house in Beverly Hills? Can you imagine Lucy telling the pilot of her Learjet to buzz the Grand Canyon so you could get a closer look while you're flying to her ski chalet in Colorado? Or imagine "stealing" silverware together from a grand New York City hotel for her new Manhattan apartment? Or staying together in a Holiday Inn in Fayetteville, North Carolina, with no closets to hang her gowns? How about taking her to the movies—she hadn't been in a Manhattan movie theater in over twenty-five years—and waiting on line to get in, in the freezing cold along with everyone else? And then she talks all the way through the film! And imagine watching Lucy catch her heel on the cuff of her pants suit and falling down the steps at the entrance to the Brasserie Restaurant on Park Avenue to the thunderous laughter of diners she barreled into headfirst? Or the best yet—imagine you're sitting in the den in her Beverly Hills mansion watching *I Love Lucy* . . . with

Lucy? Can you imagine becoming so close to a woman you had idolized from afar for so long?

There was no way to really prepare myself for the myriad perks that came with being with a famous person. Let alone, one of the most famous people in the world. Doors opened up for me literally and figuratively. As long as I was with Lucy I saw any smash Broadway musical I wanted to whether it was sold out or not. (How I wish Lucy was around for *The Producers*.) I ate in any "hot" restaurant I wanted at whatever time I wanted. In short, I was "yes-sirred" and "no-problem-sirred," and "anything-else-we-can-do-for-you-sirred" all over. I also got to meet lots of other famous people I would have otherwise never met. And these famous people were interested in who I was and what I thought and where I'd been and where I was going so long as it related to my very famous friend. People who wouldn't have given me the right time of day suddenly had lots of time to spend with me. In a sense I became famous, too. Hanging out with Lucy was a heady trip that took me to a very rarified place and I tried real hard to keep my ego in check. Because the moment my famous friend was out of sight, in everyone else's eyes I went back to just being me again. The magic, I realized, was in being with Lucy, not just knowing her. And if once in a while I felt myself taking her for granted, I would simply look at Lucy (usually across the backgammon table) and get awestruck all over again.

Lucy spent lots of time in New York. I went to Beverly Hills. We were together in Palm Springs and Snowmass. Lucy entertained military men and Harvard men and I went along. We spent the day with a prince and the night with a president. Lucy and I had a very special relationship. We were more than friends, we were family, and when given the opportunity we were inseparable. We got along famously (pun intended) all the time except for the time Lucy didn't talk to me for a year and a half, but that's another episode in this book.

Lucy didn't work very much during the early 1980s except for an occasional appearance on the *Tonight Show* or a *Bob Hope Special*. When she did work, I was with her as much as I could be. When we were together we played word games in dressing rooms, hotel rooms, and airport lounges. Lucy was the only one I knew who played Jotto in her head without pencil and paper. When we weren't together, Lucy would call me up and without even a "Hello," she would spell, "P—C—H—E—O" and I would have to mix up the letters to form a word. I would say, "Epoch," she'd call me a smart-ass and hang up. She loved to do stuff like that. Lucy was big on games and small on small talk. And once she learned how to play backgammon, she rarely played anything else. And if you didn't play along with Lucy you didn't stay very long with Lucy. It was that simple.

Lucy was very, very smart. She was not inherently funny, but funnier than she thought. "I don't think funny," she'd say to me, "You think funny. I just 'deliver the goods.' " (How's that for an understatement?) And nothing was funnier than to make Lucy laugh. She didn't just laugh, she howled. She guffawed. Her laugh made you laugh, every time. It was from way down deep in her gut and it was her stock and trademark. Once when we were playing backgammon I made her laugh so hard her upper denture dropped right out of her mouth and on to the table. Lucy didn't know what to do so without missing a beat I picked up the dice and her teeth, handed them to her and said, "I think these are yours!"

The middle of the 1980s was filled with bitter disappointment and loss for Lucy, professionally and personally. Within weeks she lost her new sitcom series and the love of her life. I don't know which devastated her more but I do know that Lucy laughed less and less and grew more and more despondent. She rarely worked or left her Beverly Hills mansion. She suffered a stroke in May of 1988 and in less than a year she was dead.

I spent a lot of time with Lucy in the last few months of her life, and I figured out more about her during that time than in all the years I had known her. In the end I finally realized why backgammon had become not just a game to pass the time but an obsession for Lucy. It was because the backgammon table became a place to exercise her artistic gifts. Just watch any *Lucy* episode and watch her genius—the wit, the spontaneity, the sensitivity, and the innate understanding of her costars. And most important of all, watch Lucy roll along with whatever was thrown at her. And if you know backgammon, you'll know that's what the game is all about— it's fast, always challenging, intensely competitive, often hilarious, and completely unpredictable—everything Lucy was and everything Lucy loved most. And besides, at the backgammon table Lucy was once again the star, and I, along with a small inner sanctum of friends and family she "entertained" were literally her supporting players. Hell, even during impromptu backgammon tournaments, whether we were on her side or not, Lucy would "direct" our every move like she probably did to so many for so many years on the set of her series. Of course, I never told Lucy my backgammon obsession theory because if I did she would have stared me down with those baby blues of hers and said something like, "Are you crazy? What the *hell* are you talking about?" Knowing full well that she knew exactly what I was talking about.

In thinking back over the time I spent with Lucy, for the

most part it was a series of episodes worthy of a situation comedy but with a bittersweet ending. Life with Lucy was an amazing, exhilarating trip; at times a difficult one to stay on board, and ultimately one that ended too soon. The blessing is that I was there for the ride.

When Lucy Met Gary

Am I happy?

No, not yet . . .

I will be.

I've been humiliated.

That's not easy for a woman.

—Lucy to TV Guide, 1960

IN THE SPRING OF 1960, WHEN I WAS
nine and Lucy was nearly forty-nine she once again graced
the cover of *TV Guide* as she had done numerous times since
the debut of the television magazine in 1953. Lucy and Desi's
second child, Desi Arnaz Jr., was on the cover of the magazine's first issue just weeks after his birth on January 19, 1953.
The headline read, LUCY'S EIGHT MILLION DOLLAR BABY, referring
to the amount of the contract Lucy and Desi had signed with
CBS to continue production on the wildly popular *I Love Lucy*
for another two years.

The latest *TV Guide* story about the reigning queen of television comedy however was a sad one. She was filing for
divorce from Desi Arnaz, her husband of nineteen years, and
the partner with whom she had created a television empire

unprecedented in size and scope for its time. Nearly two decades of womanizing, excessive drinking, and mental abuse
had taken its toll on Lucy, so after Desilu wrapped the final
episode of the *Lucy-Desi Comedy Hour*, Lucy called the sitcom and
her marriage quits. Once before in 1944, Lucy filed for divorce from Desi but changed her mind on the morning of
the court date after a rendezvous with Desi the night before.
Things were different now. The drunken stupors, the temper
tantrums in front of the kids, and the public humiliation were
more than she could bear. And yet, if you read between the
lines of the *TV Guide* story, it was clear she was still in love
with Desi. That's what made it so heartbreaking.

America was not ready for Lucy and Desi to split, under
any circumstances. Ike and Mamie Eisenhower may have still
been in the White House, but Lucy and Desi were in everybody else's house. The marriage on and off the TV screen had
become legendary and the public could not endure its shat-
tering. To the millions of fans that tuned in CBS on Monday
nights Lucy and Desi *were* Lucy and Ricky—their personal lives
and television personas were one and the same. So it was no
surprise that Lucy received literally tens of thousands of letters
begging her not to divorce Desi. To get through this very
difficult period in her life, Lucy turned to Dr. Norman Vincent
Peale, who proselytized the power of positive thinking. And
she publicly acknowledged Peale's spiritual support in getting
her through the divorce and on with her life.

Lucy wanted to, needed to get as far away from Beverly
Hills and Desi as possible, so she packed up and moved to
Manhattan with her mother, DeDe, her daughter, Lucie, Desi
Jr., and her personal assistant and chauffeur Frank Gorey. They
moved into the penthouse of the newly built Imperial House

on East Sixty-ninth Street—ironically very close to Lucy and Ricky's fictional 623 East Sixty-eighth Street address.

Lucy agreed to star in what would be her first and only Broadway musical, *Wildcat*, of which Desilu Productions was the sole backer to the tune of $400,000, a huge sum of money in 1960. The show opened first in Philadelphia to appreciative audiences but unenthusiastic critics. When it opened in New York on December 15, the opening night crowd roared with approval but the show received generally poor notices. Although disliking the show, Walter Kerr in the *New York Times* was kind to Lucy. "Miss Ball is up there doing all the spectacular and animated and energetic and deliriously accomplished things she can do." Lucy's fans poured into Broadway's Alvin Theatre by the busload, but continual ill health forced Lucy to close the show five months later in May 1961. I think the stress of doing eight shows a week and not having Desi at her side quickly did her in. She returned almost $200,000 in ticket refunds out of her own pocket.

Paula Stewart was Lucy's costar in *Wildcat*, and would remain a close friend of hers until Lucy's death. During the run of the musical, Paula was dating a stand-up comic named Jack Carter who had a friend named Gary Morton. Every night, exhausted, Lucy would go right home alone from the theater to her penthouse apartment. The last thing on Lucy's mind was men. One night Paula finally cajoled Lucy into having a late supper with her, Jack, and Gary.

Gary Morton, born Morton Goldaper in the Bronx, was fifteen years younger than Lucy. When they met, Lucy was nearly fifty. Gary had just turned thirty-five. His physical appearance and manner suggested a guy ten years older, which probably made Lucy more at ease about the vast difference in their ages, if at the time she even knew how old he really was. Gary was a stand-up comedian working the borscht belt circuit in the Catskill Mountains, and the Copacabana and Radio City Music Hall in Manhattan.

Gary Morton was 180 degrees different from Desi Arnaz. He wasn't particularly bright. He wasn't particularly talented. He certainly wasn't rich. He was a second-rate comic who until he met Lucy could not even land a guest appearance on *The Ed Sullivan Show*. But on the plus side, Gary was sober, steady, and he could make Lucy laugh. And those were qualities sorely missing in Lucy's life. Gary used to tell gossip queens Hedda Hopper and Louella Parsons that he wasn't in awe of Lucy when he met her because he worked nights and slept all day so he never watched I *Love Lucy* and didn't know how famous Lucy was. It made for good press and you could be sure Lucy approved the items before they were printed.

Lucy and Gary hit it off at dinner and started seeing each other, until *Wildcat* closed. Lucy liked his slight irreverence; but don't worry, when they were together he knew who Lucy was. When Lucy returned to Beverly Hills after a much-needed holiday in England and Italy—after *Wildcat* closed—Gary followed her out west. I was distantly related to Gary Morton (I'll explain later), so I was beside myself with joy when I heard Lucy and Gary were dating. One day I was walking with my mother on White Plains Road in the Bronx and we met Gary's mother, Rose Goldaper, on the street. She was a very funny and bawdy woman who if she chose to could have been a great vaudevillian in her day. So there she was standing on the street corner kvelling (Yiddish for bragging) about her son Gary, and how she had prayed every night that he would find himself someone nice to marry, somebody good, and maybe this time her prayers would be answered. I was ten years old and I remember thinking to myself, "Is she kidding, someone *nice*, somebody *good*, this is Lucille Ball she's talking about, not a Rockette!" Gary had been married once to the sister of Judith Exner. Judith was one of President Kennedy's mistresses, who went public about her relationship with JFK shortly before her death. Gary's marriage to Exner was annulled. I never knew why and the family never spoke about it.

As we walked away I said to my mother, "Can you imagine if Lucy marries Gary and becomes part of our family?" My mother laughed, took my hand, and told me not to think about it too much. Was everyone in the family surprised, probably none more than Mama Rose herself when Lucille Ball married Morton Goldaper at the Marble Collegiate Church in New York on November 19, 1961. As thousands of fans lined the streets behind police barricades hoping to get a glimpse of the new Mrs. Gary Morton, Lucy's friend, the Reverend Norman Vincent Peale married them. Lucille Ball Morton was now officially a member of our family, although my mother predicted the marriage would not last six months. She was right. It lasted nearly twenty-eight years.

Gary moved into the colonial house at 1000 North Roxbury Drive in Beverly Hills, California just shy of his thirty-sixth birthday. He finally gave Lucy what she needed most—marital stability, happiness, and a home life. And Lucy gave him what he needed most—polish, cachet, financial security, and steady employment when he became the producer for her new television series *The Lucy Show*.

Desi had sold his share of Desilu to Lucy in 1962 for just over two and a half million dollars, and at forty-five years of age he "retired" to Del Mar, California. Lucy was now the executive in charge of production of her new series as well as *The Untouchables*. She was also renting production space for *Ben*

Casey, The Andy Griffith Show, My Three Sons, My Favorite Martian, and *The Danny Thomas Show* with Danny often referring to Lucy as "my favorite landlady!"

Contrary to what has been written about Lucy, her business acumen was not her forte. By virtue of her divorce from Desi and her subsequent purchase of the studio, Lucy was thrust into a position of bureaucratic power that she found neither comfortable nor enviable. As executive producer of *I Love Lucy,* Desi Arnaz had made virtually all the business production and financial decisions leaving Lucy to do what she did better than anybody else—make people laugh. Now she had to oversee the production of a couple of top Neilsen-rated shows and sometimes she had to do what she hated to do more than anything else—fire people. In the meantime, Gary was learning the business, warming up Lucy's studio audience every week, and doing what he was told.

For Gary's hard work, loyalty, efficiency, and devotion he was rewarded. He loved vintage cars, so Lucy bought him a Stutz Bearcat. He loved good clothing, so Lucy got him a brand-new, very expensive wardrobe. He loved to play golf, so Lucy saw to it that he became a member of the prestigious Brentwood Country Club in Los Angeles. And although Gary enjoyed living in Beverly Hills, he loved the house in Palm Springs that he now shared with Lucy.

Lucy was also incredibly generous to Gary's family. She opened her homes and guest houses to Gary's mother, Rose, and Gary's sister, Helen, who frequently came out from back east for extended stays in Beverly Hills and Palm Springs. Lucy bought Rose a full-length mink coat that she proudly wore *inside* the studio on the *Hy Gardner Show* when he hosted a program about celebrity mothers-in-law. In fact shortly after they were married Lucy told Rose how happy Gary had made her and that she would give Gary anything he wanted, but if she found him even looking at another woman, she'd kill him. Over the years Gary accrued his own personal wealth working for Lucille Ball Productions and investing wisely. He, too, was very generous to his sister and his mother, buying them condominiums in New York, Miami Beach, and West Hollywood. Lucy's sister-in-law, Helen, moved to California in the middle of the 1970s after her husband died and became a companion and confidante to Lucy.

In the last decade of Lucy's life, Gary befriended oil billionaire Marvin Davis, who bought 20th Century Fox Pictures. Soon after, Lucille Ball Productions moved onto the Fox lot and Gary became the executive producer on his first and only major motion picture, a mediocre film called *All the Right Moves* starring a relatively unknown actor named Tom Cruise. In the years that followed, Gary mostly played golf, read scripts, and gave Lucy some really bad professional advice.

A couple of years after Lucy died Gary moved out of the house in Beverly Hills, and into his Palm Springs home. Subsequently, he married a much younger woman named Susie, who loved to play golf. Gary died of lung cancer in 1999 at the age of seventy-three, and Susie still lives in the house that Desi built for Lucy almost half a century ago.

When Lucy Met Lee

IN 1961 I WAS ELEVEN YEARS OLD
and absolutely nuts about Lucy. I'm not sure if every kid my
age felt the same way but I could not get enough of her. I
don't know if I remember first-run episodes of I *Love Lucy*
that ended in 1957, but I do remember watching the *Lucy-Desi
Comedy Hour*, which aired until April 1960. After that I watched
Lucy rerun after rerun that seemed to run night and day.

After *Lucy* ceased production Lucy had gone to New York
to do the Broadway musical *Wildcat* and began dating Gary
Morton. Gary Morton's sister Helen's husband, Bob, was my
father's first cousin, so although Gary was technically not related to me, where I came from we called it *meshpucha*, a Yiddish word for family. So when Lucy and Gary got married,
Lucy became *meshpucha*, too.

I first met Lucy in New York in the winter of 1962, shortly
after their wedding. Lucy and Gary came to Matthews Avenue
in the Bronx to visit Helen and her family, and I was invited
to the house after dinner. I lived around the corner and although I had the flu with a temperature of 102 degrees I got
up and went. I remember riding in the elevator and rehears-
ing how to introduce myself to Lucy. "Hello, Miss Ball,"

too formal I thought. "Hi Lucy," too familiar. "Hello, Mrs. Morton," too Jewish. It didn't matter. I took one look at her and uttered not a single word the whole evening. I didn't eat anything. I didn't drink anything. I just sat and stared. This was my first *I Love Lucy* episode and I felt like Lucy Ricardo when she could not take her eyes off William Holden at the Brown Derby. Lucy was teaching Helen a card game called crazy eight's and Gary was bragging about how much Lucy had won at the crap tables on a recent trip to Las Vegas. Lucy made me sit next to her, and every so often she tickled my ribs and made some Donald Duck quacks in my ear. Lucy wanted me to have a picture taken of the two of us but they ran out of film, and Lucy got very angry with Gary. I remember thinking that without a snapshot, none of my friends would believe I really was with Lucy. Hell, I didn't believe I really was there. By the time my brother picked me up outside Helen's apartment building at ten o'clock, I was delirious. I didn't know if it was high fever or just high on Lucy. It was an evening I will never forget.

When I was seventeen I saw Lucy again at Helen's son's wedding in a synagogue on Long Island. When word spread that Lucy was coming, probably from the caterer themselves, the whole town of Woodmere, New York, came out to greet her. I felt sorry for the bride who was so upstaged at her own wedding. I remember introducing Lucy to my eighty-six-year-old grandfather, Max, who asked, "Lucy who?" He then asked her what she did for a living.

I saw Lucy once again in Las Vegas when I was twenty-two. She and Gary asked Helen and her family and me out for a long weekend. Frank Sinatra was checking out of the six-bedroom duplex suite and we were checking in. I had a terrific time. Other than on those three occasions I saw Lucy on television along with the rest of America.

In the winter of 1980, my partner Tom Wells and I vacationed on the island of Kauai, then stopped off in Los Angeles on our way back to New York. Over the years I had remained very close to Gary's sister, Helen, and it was she who suggested that when I get to California I call Gary and Lucy to say hello. I had not seen them for almost eight years. Lucy was no longer doing her weekly sitcom; in fact Lucy wasn't doing much of anything except staying home and playing Scrabble with some close friends. And learning to play a new game called backgammon, which she loved from her first roll of the dice, but could not master as quickly as the word games at which she excelled. I called Gary and he invited us over. "Lucy's taking a backgammon lesson but she'll be done by eight, we'll have dessert."

Tom and I arrived at 1000 North Roxbury Drive in Beverly Hills at eight on the button. Actually, we came by at seven-thirty and circled the block a couple dozen times, seeking out movie stars and checking out the houses. We rang the front doorbell and Gary answered. Before I had the chance to introduce Tom to Gary at the doorstep, a voice bellowed from the other side of the grand foyer, "Gary, why the *hell* don't you let them in?" It was unmistakably Lucy. We walked through the center hall and into what looked like a den, but which Lucy called her lanai. It was Lucy, *in person*, dressed in black from head to toe save for the shock of orange hair that was also unmistakably Lucy. She looked beautiful. And she looked younger than a woman in her late sixties. She extended her hand to Tom and said, "Hi, I'm Lucy." I don't know why, but I said, "No shit," and she broke up. What do you know, I made Lucy laugh.

We spent the night talking about everything and everybody except me. She wanted to know all about Tom. Where he came from, Memphis. Where he went to school, Harvard. What he did for a living, advertising. What his parents did. How many brothers and sisters he had. When I tried to talk about me, Lucy told me to keep quiet, she was talking to Tom. It was another episode of I Love Lucy—the one where Lucy brings Ethel together with a new friend of hers and the new friend and Ethel get real chummy and leave Lucy out completely. This time I was Lucy.

We stayed for about an hour. Lucy was tired. She asked us to come back the next night for dinner, but unfortunately we had to get back to our jobs in Manhattan. She thought that was a flimsy excuse and said she would write us a note or call our boss and ask if we could stay on a while. Lucy was dead serious but we politely declined her offer. She said she was coming east in a few weeks and could we get together? I told her I would have to check my calendar and my secretary would get back to her. She laughed like Lucy Ricardo. We all hugged and then we said good-bye. "No 'good-bye's,' we never say 'good-bye,' " Lucy said. She walked with us down the driveway to the car admonishing me to drive carefully. As we drove off I said "Lucy, we had such a great time tonight. Thank you so much, you're the best." "No shit!" she yelled back.

On the drive back to our hotel I thought about how Lucy and I had reacquainted at a time in our lives that seemed so right for us both. I think that's why we clicked. I was twenty-nine years old, been married for almost eight years, recently divorced, and although I was now in a successful new (in more ways than one) relationship, I was still very unsure of where certain life paths were leading. Although my parents were cognizant of my lifestyle and totally accepting of Tom, my relationship with them was somewhat tenuous.

Lucy, too, in a sense was choosing new paths in her life, having neither a television series nor a television empire to occupy her time. She also wasn't particularly close to her kids, Lucie and Desi Jr. As a matter of fact, I could count the number of times I saw either of them with Lucy during the last decade of her life. All I know is that on the few occasions mother and daughter were together things always seemed a bit tense and they tended to disagree on almost everything important.

And I remember one visit to the house from Desi Jr. when Tom and I were in Beverly Hills. It was in the mid 1980s and Desi Jr. was getting his life straightened out after years of alcohol and drug abuse. He was sober, happy, and about to star in a play, *Sunday in New York*, at the Coconut Grove Playhouse in Florida. We were all sitting around the dinner table listening to Desi talk enthusiastically about his life and future when Lucy literally cut him off in mid-sentence and said it was time to play backgammon. So the next thing you know Tom, Lucy, and I are playing in the lanai and Desi is sitting alone in the dining room. I felt so sorry for Desi, and could not for the life of me understand why Lucy had seemingly so little time or patience for her own son.

Suffice it to say that for Lucie and Desi Jr., growing up in the shadow of a superstar mom whose work meant more to her than anything or anyone else could not have been easy. When they were teenagers trying to have their own show business career, yet forever being the children of America's most famous couple, I'm sure it led to familial dysfunction. My God, they even had the same first names as their parents.

Maybe Lucy and I were at a juncture that gave us a common

bond, which linked us as "mother and son" without all the baggage that encumbers almost any *real* mother-son relationship, famous or otherwise. All I knew was that she was totally accepting of who I was, who Tom was, and who we were together. And I also knew that from that night on Lucy was going to play an integral part in my life and I in hers. Was I being realistic, who knows, or was I just being swept into a fantasy from spending an hour or so with this remarkable woman?

Lucy Plays the Palace

A FEW WEEKS AFTER WE CAME HOME I received a phone call at my office from Wanda Clark. Wanda had been Lucy's secretary since 1963, a couple of years after she married Gary. Wanda knew a lot, had seen a lot, but always said very little. She was warm, friendly, witty, and bright, and loyal to Lucy to the nth degree. I had never met Wanda, but when I was a kid if I wanted to send Lucy a Christmas or birthday gift or something I would call Wanda. She'd always make me feel like I was Lucy's number one fan.

"Lucy and Gary are coming to New York on the twenty-eighth for a week," she said. "Lucy is leaving CBS and signing a new contract with NBC and has lots of interviews, but Lucy wants to see you. Now hold on Lee, I'm going to put you through to the house." The next thirty seconds were an eternity. And then came the voice. "Listen, I hope you boys learned how to play backgammon by now, and you better get your asses out of work because I'm bringing my board with me. One more thing, you know everybody in New York, so get Gary and me a suite with two bedrooms in any hotel other than the Sherry Netherland, Jeeesus that hotel is falling apart, and get us a car and driver, and it doesn't have to be a stretch limousine, and I can't talk with you any more because Gaby is here to give me another goddamn backgammon lesson, Jeeesus I'll never learn that game." Click. Dial tone. "Hello?" I said. "Lucy? Wanda?"

Tom and I were working for a theatrical advertising agency named Ash LeDonne. Our clients included Broadway and Off-Broadway shows, Radio City Music Hall, Resorts International Hotel Casino in Atlantic City, and Helmsley Hotels. Tom was a vice president in charge of marketing and I was a creative director. Our offices were right next door to each other, so when I finished talking to Lucy, actually, when Lucy got finished talking to me (since I never did a get a word in "etchwise," as Ricky Ricardo used to say), I ran in and told Tom that Lucy was coming to town.

"Hey, I got an idea," Tom said, "Let's put her up at The Helmsley Palace." Our agency had just been awarded the Helmsley account, not so much on the merit of our advertising pitch, but for a personal favor Tom did for Leona Helmsley. After our presentation was over Leona told us that in a few days she was throwing her annual "I'm just wild about Harry" party for her multibillionaire husband Harry and the theme was "The Wizard of Ours"; Harry of course was the wizard. Leona needed a "yellow brick road" to lead the guests from cocktails, which were being held in their penthouse apartment at The Park Lane Hotel, into the elevator and down to the ballroom where the dinner dance would take place. Tom's father was a designer, the first interior decorator for Holiday Inns worldwide, and Tom assured Leona that his dad could get a carpet made with a yellow brick stencil and have it delivered to the hotel in time for the party. "You get me that carpet, and you got the account," Leona croaked. Seventy-two hours later Leona got her "yellow brick road" and we got the business. As it turned out, we got "the business" from Leona in more ways than one.

We called the general manager of The Helmsley Palace, and luckily it was the same general manager who was there a few weeks earlier when we were awarded the account. Leona Helmsley was tyrannical and fired employees on less than a whim. She was known to so berate hotel executives in public as to leave them cowering in their Gucci's. "The Queen of Mean," as the *New York Post* nicknamed her also didn't believe in paying taxes, which she said were only for the "little people." So Leona herself wound up doing a little time with people in a minimum security prison in Danbury, Connecticut, conveniently located just a few miles from her palatial Greenwich estate.

The manager reserved a two-bedroom suite for Lucy and Gary under the name of Morton, on the forty-sixth floor of the Tower Suite portion of The Helmsley Palace. It was a beautiful traditionally furnished suite with two huge bedrooms, each with its own bath and dressing room with lots of closets, a living room, dining room, full kitchen, with all windows overlooking St. Patrick's Cathedral.

Our advertising agency was at 1500 Broadway, right in the heart of Times Square, where *Good Morning America* is now televised from studios on the ground floor. Almost every night after work Tom and I would head over to the upstairs bar at Sardi's a block away on West Forty-fourth Street. Lots of producers, directors, actors, and press agents hung out there, and we landed more accounts at the Sardi's bar than we did in our own boardroom.

One snowy winter night shortly before Lucy came to town, we couldn't get a cab from Sardi's so we hailed a passing limousine. The driver was a man named Ambrose. The chocolate brown limo with cream interior was standard size; Ambrose was not. He was a burly Irish guy with a big smile and bad teeth and an easy way about him, and you could tell right off that he loved his work. We started chatting and Ambrose dropped names of the celebrities he chauffeured around and told us that he drove Sarah Vaughn whenever she was in New York. "I drop everything when Sassy's in town." He said he was a much better and safer driver than all those other "dirt bag" drivers around town. "Dirt bag" was one of his favorite expressions. By the time we got to our apartment I told him that Lucille Ball was coming to town in a few days and if he wanted to, he could pick her up at JFK and drive her around Manhattan. He looked in the rearview, laughingly called us "dirt bags," accused us of being "shit faced," took our money, and gave us his card: Ambrose Hartley. Chauffeur. We opened our own door and left. The next day I called our new chauffeur friend and told him Lucy really *was* coming to town, and I was going out on a limb asking him to drive her since I didn't know him at all. "C'mon 'dirt bag,' give me a shot."

Ambrose, Tom, and I picked up Lucy and Gary at the airport and Ambrose became their New York driver for the next seven years. Lucy adored Ambrose and she gave him money to fix his teeth, and she bought him new clothes and a chauffeur's cap, and she made him go on a diet to lose weight. Ambrose loved Lucy. He would buy her lilacs in the spring—her favorite flower—and take her to the Food Emporium and for walks in Central Park when I wasn't around, and his wife would bake cookies for Gary and knit sweaters for Lucy's grandchildren. Ambrose even had special New York license plates put on his limousine that read I LOVE LUCY.

Then one day Gary fired Ambrose, just like that, because he thought Ambrose was overcharging them. He convinced

Lucy that Ambrose was ripping them off, padding the bills with more hours than he actually worked. It was preposterous and I told Gary and Lucy so, but it didn't matter. Ambrose was gone, and from then on they never had a regular driver in New York.

Lucy loved her suite at the Helmsley Palace. It was comfortable with big cushy sofas and armchairs that both she and Gary liked. It was clean, and the room service was very prompt. Leona would have it no other way. And neither would Lucy. When we arrived, the first things she unpacked were her backgammon board, which she ordered Tom to set up, and her cigarette snuffers, which she got me to place in all the available ashtrays in the suite. Then she said to call room service and get a card table to put the board on. "Tell them it's for Lucille Ball," she hollered as she went into the master bedroom to unpack her clothes. Gary went into the other bedroom to unpack his clothes and toiletries. They always slept in the same bedroom.

After a few minutes she came back into the living room. She was wearing a pale blue jogging suit with a big embroidered L over the left breast. She wore matching colored flats on her feet. There was a handkerchief-style white scarf around her neck and her hair color, in perfect contrast to her outfit, was more orange than I had remembered. She wore big, slightly tinted blue, tortoiseshell-framed prescription glasses that set off her blue, blue eyes. She carried a small white pocketbook shaped like a workman's lunch pail in one hand and literally a "baggie" in the other hand that was filled with one-dollar bills.

"C'mon, let's play" she ordered. "Aren't you tired from the flight or hungry?" I asked. "It's only six o'clock in the evening California time, and besides I ate my way across country.

Now, are we going to play or not?" "Yes, sir," I said and saluted. Lucy laughed, sort of. Tom and I were very nervous. We were playing backgammon with Lucille Ball. Just *being* with Lucy was a nerve-wracking experience. We had bought a beginner's book on backgammon and we were teaching ourselves at home. In the meantime Lucy was taking lessons from Gaby Horowitz, a world champion backgammon player who immigrated from Israel and was now making the rounds of Beverly Hills winning scads of money from rich matrons eager to learn the game.

We sat around the card table that was delivered very quickly to the suite. Lucy accused Tom of setting up the board wrong, so she reset it exactly as it had been set. This made me nervous, and Tom upset. Clearly Lucy *needed* to be in charge. We rolled for who was to play the chouette (a game where one person plays against two, but only one of the partners roll the dice at the table). Tom would be "in the box" playing alone against Lucy and me, but Lucy would be sitting out. I won the first game with little advice from my famous partner, who could hardly sit still. She was popping up and down, rearranging furniture in the suite, putting on gobs of lipstick, and laughing a lot at just about everything I said. I could tell she was very happy to be where she was, and I think a little nervous, too.

"All right, Lucy, you're up," I said and Lucy sat down in Tom's place. Now I was "in the box," playing against Lucy and Tom. This time Lucy set up the board completely backward but Tom and I didn't say anything, just quickly reset it when Lucy got up to answer the phone.

"Yes," Lucy said in a bass octave dead-on unintentional imitation of Harvey Fierstein. "Thank you very much, yes, I am very glad to be back east," she continued, winking at us, who were conspicuously staring at her. "Everything is wonderful, just perfect, thank you." Lucy continued, impatiently wanting to get back to the game, "Tell me dear, what's your name?" Pause. "Leona. Pause. Leona what?" I started wildly flailing in my seat. "Oh, Helmsley!" Lucy deadpanned, making one of those contorted gestures with her mouth that Lucy Ricardo used to make when she was caught doing something naughty. Then Lucy "saved" the day by bursting out laughing and telling Leona that of course she knew it was she all the time. Lucy thanked Leona for calling and Tom and I applauded, while Lucy graciously took a bow. "Good *God*, what a bore," Lucy said. "Let's play backgammon!"

So there we were, as it were—Lucy and her boys playing the Palace. The world's most famous redhead shaking her backgammon cup and rolling out the dice with one hand, chain-smoking her Philip Morris with the other. Sometimes inhaling, sometimes not, blowing smoke like a star. It was tough to concentrate on the game. None of us were good players, but that did not stop Lucy from giving advice on how to make just about every move or when to use the doubling cube. Most of the time she had no idea what she was talking about. Of course, she had learned from one of the champs so I was totally intimidated and when she was my partner, I listened to her and we almost always lost.

Tom was not as starstruck as me in the first place, and in the second place he wanted to play his own game, even when Lucy was his partner. So when Lucy said to make this move, if Tom disagreed he'd make that move. When Lucy wanted him to give me the doubling cube to raise the stakes, Tom would say it was too early in the game. This did not please Lucy at all and finally she could not contain herself. "Jeeesus Tom, when the *hell* are you going to listen to me and learn how to play this game. You've got an ego the size of this suite!" Tom's cheeks grew the color of Lucy's hair. We finished the game in silence. Tom won.

It was getting late and Lucy was tired and Tom was angry. Although Tom didn't think so at the time, I knew that Lucy knew she had hurt his feelings. But as I would learn later on in our friendship, Lucy rarely if ever apologized for her behavior. "Let's settle up," Lucy said as she opened her "baggie" full of dollar bills. "I think the Harvard guy gets all our money. You know what they say, you can tell a Harvard man, but you can't tell him much." We all started laughing, but it was forced. Tom declined the money and said we should keep a running tally. "God, I've got so many interviews tomorrow and they'll all ask the same Goddamn questions over and over again. Come over for dinner at six we'll call in room service and play," Lucy ordered rather than asked. I quickly suggested we eat dinner out instead to which Lucy abruptly replied, "Dinner out, are you out of your mind!" Then she kissed us good night, said no good-bye, and closed the door.

Tom and I rode down the elevator and neither of us said a word. As we walked in silence for blocks up Park Avenue toward our apartment on a freezing January night, I finally broke the ice and said, "What an incredible night, do you believe we were actually with Lucille Ball, just the three of us, wasn't that so much fun?"

"I don't care if she is your seventh cousin, three times removed," Tom said softly, matter-of-factly, "and I don't care if she is the biggest star in the whole universe, I am not going back there."

I laughed it off. "Don't be ridiculous," I said, "That's the way Lucy is."

"Uh-oh, you go, I'm staying home."

I couldn't say I blamed Tom for his visceral reaction to Lucy. I had heard stories throughout the years about Lucy frequently lambasting colleagues on her set when she did her series, but I never saw it with my own eyes. But anyway, this was different. This wasn't work, this was just a game of back-gammon, so why would she get so upset? Or was it more than a game to Lucy? Was Lucy's newfound fixation on the roll of a dice replacing her obsession with the television career she no longer had? It was too early in my friendship with Lucy to say for sure but I did think her behavior with Tom was inappropriate to say the least. And, I sensed that she was also testing Tom. Did he have the mettle to stand up to her? Or was he going to be just another "supporting player" who she could boss around at whim? And when Tom did stand up to her, did Lucy herself have what it took to be the best back-gammon player she could be? Or unlike her brilliant career, would Lucy not be at the top of this game?

Later in our relationship I learned that Lucy could be con-trary for no apparent reason, which could have also accounted for the way she treated Tom. If she asked you what time you wanted lunch and you said noon, she'd say, "Who the *hell* eats lunch at noon—we'll eat at twelve-thirty." Lucy could be cantankerous. One time she argued with me over the proper way to toast an English muffin. Can you imagine? It would have been laughable enough for a *Lucy* episode if she wasn't so angry at the time.

Lucy could also be stubborn. It was her way or the high-way. You never won an argument with Lucy and if you were smart you wouldn't even start one. And if Lucy didn't know how to do something, she assumed nobody else did either.

These character flaws surfaced only in private and to the most trusting of her friends and family. In all the years I knew

Lucy, in the public eye she was never less than charming, considerate, appreciative, and loving. And she never publicly talked badly about anybody she worked with or who worked for her in the business. Except for the story Lucy would now and then tell about how she would have fired Joan Crawford off the set of her show for coming to work drunk each day of rehearsal if Gary had not calmed Lucy down and persuaded her to finish out the week and get the episode in the can. "God, that woman was a bitch," Lucy would say.

After much cajoling from me, Tom did come back for a second night of backgammon. I told him that it wasn't every day we had a chance to get chummy with an icon. "I promise if Lucy behaves that way toward you again, we'll leave, and cultivate a friendship with another legend."

That second night Lucy was a different person, at least as far as Tom was concerned. He could do no wrong around the backgammon table, and she laughed at everything he said, and Tom is not all that funny. "Isn't this swell," I said, "Tom and Lucy and Lee—together again at the Palace. It sounds like a vaudeville act."

"Except you got the billing wrong," she shot back.

Gary went to dinner with his pal Lew Rudin, a billionaire who owns a lot of Manhattan real estate. He left as soon as we got to the suite, and he asked us to stay until he got back. Lucy told me to call room service and to order anything we wanted for dinner, and then told us *exactly* what we should eat. I ordered under the name of Mrs. Gary Morton as Lucy instructed me to, and when the food didn't come after we finished three games of backgammon, Lucy picked up the phone, called room service, and told them it was Lucille Ball in room 4601 and she was hungry. The food came up almost before she could put the receiver down, followed by two calls from the general manager and one from the head of room service to make sure everything was satisfactory.

We ate in record-breaking time. There was no need to transfer the food from the cart to the dining table, since we would only have to transfer the empty plates back onto the cart—Lucy wanted the cart out of the suite and into the hallway immediately after dinner. "God, I don't want any of those bellboys or whoever coming in here and staring at me." Who could blame her the way she looked that night in her white Helmsley Palace terry robe, with pink bunny slippers on her feet that you could see she must have had for a very, very long time, and her hair up in rollers.

We played backgammon until after midnight. Lucy was playing better, concentrating more, although still telling us what to do—but in a nicer way, and we were all much more relaxed. For the next ten nights, until Lucy finished her New York engagement at the Palace, we called room service, played backgammon, and made Lucy laugh a lot.

Lucy in Beverly Hills

LUCY WENT BACK HOME AND I WENT back to just being me. While Lucy was in New York I saw virtually nobody except Tom and that was because we lived together and saw Lucy together. Lucy was not ready to meet my friends yet nor was I ready for them to meet her.

Less than a month after Lucy had gone home, I got a phone call from Wanda. "What airline do you boys like to fly?"

"Wanda, why?"

"Lucy wants you to fly out for the long Memorial Day weekend."

"Wanda," I said, "Tell Lucy we would love to but we have plans."

"Honey, that's something you're going to have to tell her yourself. Hold on, I'll put you through to the house."

"This is Lucille Ball. What do you mean, you have plans? Get your asses out here!" Wanda had told her, but it didn't matter, Lucy was not going to take no for an answer. In fact Lucy rarely took "no" for an answer from anybody, although it was one of her favorite responses.

I had to admit the invitation to stay at Lucy's home in Beverly Hills was a tough one to turn down. We had personal and business commitments in New York that we couldn't break so Tom stayed home and I went by myself.

Wanda arranged for my ticket. I paid for it. I left on the Thursday before Memorial Day. Lucy ordered me to take the earliest flight out of JFK. That way I could get to the house, unpack, have lunch early enough to still get in at least five hours of backgammon before we had dinner where we watched *Wheel of Fortune* (Lucy loved Vanna White), *Jeopardy!* (Lucy loved Alex Trebeck), then play more backgammon and go to sleep. Lucy gave me implicit travel instructions, which Wanda conveyed to me on the phone. I should pack light with only casual clothes since we weren't going out anywhere fancy and not check any baggage so that I could get out of LAX faster. I should take a cab to the house. There was no need to rent a car because I would not need one, which made me happy because I assumed I would drive one of Gary's four cars that sat in the garage. Lastly, when I got to the house I should ring the side doorbell, by the driveway because that was the door that friends and family used. Lucy was also very superstitious so Wanda said that if I did use the front door to get in I would always have to use the front door to get out. I asked no questions, just wrote all the instructions down on paper so I wouldn't forget and did what I was told.

Lucy's home on Roxbury Drive sat at the corner of Roxbury and Lexington, one block North of Sunset Boulevard. Jimmy Stewart's house occupied a double lot adjacent to Lucy's on Roxbury Drive on the other side of Lexington. Jack Benny had lived right next door to Lucy but sold the house in the early seventies, a couple of years before his death. Rosemary Clooney lived across the street, as did Ira Gershwin's widow. Peter Falk lived up the street. The homes were right off the street—very accessible to people walking by. Except nobody *walked* by in Beverly

Hills. The lots the homes were built on were deeper than they were wide, so as you drove on Roxbury Drive it looked like a street in your typical upper-class suburban neighborhood, except most of the neighbors were entertainment legends.

I got to the house around noon, after rereading my instructions in the cab on the way into Beverly Hills, and went to the side door. I peeked through the locked wrought iron gates that led to the pool and guesthouse. A big sign hung over the gates that read BEWARE OF DOG. In front of the door was a mat with an initial G on it. I thought for a moment then realized it stood for Goldaper. It made me laugh out loud.

I rang the bell and after a minute or so Lucy opened it herself. The "guard" dog was a four-pound white toy poodle named Tinker yapping and scampering about her feet. Lucy's hair was brushed away from her face, and the color matched the fruit on the trees in her backyard. She wore a black jogging suit with Lucy embroidered on the left sleeve. Lucy looked gorgeous. Lucy *always* looked gorgeous. "Jeeesus, I thought you'd never get here!" she exclaimed, enveloping me in her arms.

As I broke from the embrace I asked her if she wore her name on her sleeve so that people would know who she is. "No," Lucy replied. "It's so that I remember who I am." I couldn't tell if she meant that as a joke or not.

I dropped my bags just inside the hallway and Lucy gave me a tour of the house. I thought, How many people in those dozens of tour buses that cruised by Lucy's house from morning to night would have given their right arm for a tour of the inside, let alone by Lucy herself? Then I laughingly thought, Maybe I could give tours when Lucy was asleep and pick up a few bucks.

It was very quiet except for the sound of a game show coming from a distant television set. It was Thursday and Kum and Choo the Chinese couple who were live-in help were off. Lucy said Gary was at the office, or more likely at Hillcrest playing golf. Frank Gorey was out running some errands. Frank was Lucy's driver, when she wanted one. He was also her personal assistant, confidante, and I think considered by Lucy to be part of the family. He worked for Lucy since the middle 1950s and he used to drive Lucy's mom, DeDe, who passed away in 1977. Michael Maurer, who was Gary's sister Helen's son (my third cousin), worked also for Lucy but he was not around.

We walked down the hall past the servant's quarters and I peaked into the laundry room which also doubled for Lucy's makeshift beauty salon, complete with professional hair washing sink, professional dryer, and boxes of henna rinse stacked up next to boxes of Tide detergent. The end of the hallway led to the kitchen, which was larger than the Ricardo's but with wallpaper, countertops and appliances that looked equally 1950s. There was something cooking on the stove. It smelled delicious and I was hungry.

Lucy led me into Gary's den, which was just past the kitchen on the right before you got to the front hallway and foyer. It was a cozy room with upholstered chairs and ottomans and a leather sofa. One wall was lined with floor to ceiling shelves of videotapes of all the *Lucy* shows, plus cassettes of other shows where she had made guest appearances and the movies she made that were available on tape. A console television set occupied one corner of the den. Over the fireplace mantle was a marvelous color portrait of Lucy which was painted by the actress Claire Trevor, and on the opposite wall was a painting of Lucie and Desi Jr. done when they were young children. There were framed autographed photos inscribed to Lucy and to Lucy and Desi from among others Buster Keaton, Maurice Chevalier, Frank Sinatra, and Jack Benny. The bay windows faced Roxbury

Drive and were covered with natural-wood shutters. Perpendicular to the windows was Gary's magnificent antique mahogany desk and chair. There was a Rolodex on the desk, which was filled with the home and office phone numbers of just about every Hollywood star.

Across from the den was the dining room, an informal room with a large white Formica table with eight white cane-back chairs with lemon yellow vinyl cushions. There was a white sideboard with hideous yellow and green artificial flowers in a yellow porcelain bowl on top of it and a couple of fake ficus trees flanking the windows. Near the door to the kitchen was a Plexiglas television stand with a seventeen-inch television. The windows of the dining room faced the back gardens and pool. Half-buried in the olive green shag carpet, under the chair at the head of the table was a buzzer, which I imagined Lucy used to summon the staff at dinnertime. Just like in the *Lucy-Desi Comedy Hour*, where Lucy invites Tallulah Bankhead for dinner and wants to impress her, so she hires Fred and Ethel as staff and summons them constantly with a floor buzzer.

Lucy and I were now in the center foyer just inside the front doorway where I first met Lucy back in January. As you faced the back of the house, off to the right of the foyer was a formal living room that Lucy and Gary rarely used except for an occasional interview or photo shoot. The furniture was all French provincial except for a custom-made backgammon table that was created from a regulation-size card table and had thick black wooden legs. The wall adjacent to the backgammon table had floor to ceiling bookcases filled with leather bound *Lucy* scripts. All 179 *I Love Lucy* episodes plus the *Lucy Desi-Comedy Hour* programs as well as *The Lucy Show* and *Here's Lucy*. There were over five hundred original scripts in all.

In back of the foyer and just to the right of a spiral stairway, which led up to the bedrooms, was the lanai. It was a very large room, with lots of upholstered furniture; two divans, two love seats, three club chairs with matching ottomans. On one wall was a television and stereo combination console like the ones popular in the 1960s and which looked like it was probably purchased then. Right above it hung a huge remarkably lifelike oil portrait of Gary swinging a golf club, which was painted by Fred Williams, a makeup artist from Desilu days. In the windowed corner adjacent to the console was another custom-made backgammon table like the one in the living room, except this one had white legs with three cane-back Formica chairs identical to the dining room chairs.

This small corner of the lanai was where Lucy spent more time than anywhere in the entire house—playing backgammon. In fact, the backgammon table, chairs, and surrounding furniture are now replicated at the Lucy exhibits at both Universal Studio in Los Angeles, and in Orlando, Florida, so millions of her fans can get a glimpse at where Lucy spent most of the last decade of her life. Behind the back wall of the lanai was a projection room. From there Lucy and Gary showed thirty-five millimeter prints of current films on a screen that, with a push of a button, lowered from the ceiling just in front of the console. There was a wall of sliding glass doors, which led to the gardens, the pool, and the guest and pool houses.

Lucy walked me out into the gardens and toward the guesthouse, which was adjacent to the pool. Everywhere I looked there were orange and lemon trees, rose bushes, and pots of impatiens. The pool was kidney shaped and heated to eighty degrees. There was a small trickling waterfall at one end. It was late spring in Beverly Hills, the "gray days" as Lucy called them, and the early afternoon sun was just breaking through the cloud-filled sky, so typical of the weather pattern that time of year.

We walked into the guesthouse where I would be staying. The house was really one large room with a small dressing room, bathroom, and kitchenette. The room had two full-size beds separated by a night table and lamp. The headboards were huge and fully upholstered in a gold damask material. The bedspreads matched the draperies, which were fully drawn across the bay windows. The carpeting was wall to wall gold shag. The dressers, writing table, and chair were all mahogany. The bathroom was Pepto-Bismol pink—the sink, toilet, tile, and bathtub. There was no stove in the kitchen, just a couple of portable burners and a half refrigerator. An old-fashioned toaster sat on the countertop and inside the cupboards were Melmac plates and a few mismatched glasses. All over the room there were baby pictures of Lucy and it looked and felt like a room she might have grown up in back in Celoron, New York, just outside of Jamestown. The guest house was rather dark and a bit dank, with the only sunlight coming through the small bathroom windows. As Lucy showed me around the room, opening drawers and closets and instructing me on what to put where, I thought about Desi Jr. and Liza Minnelli, who holed up in this guesthouse for weeks at a time while they were briefly engaged in the early 1970s.

Lucy took me through a door in the kitchenette, which opened on to a storage room—a room that looked like it might have one day long ago been a garage. I stepped inside. Lucy stood back and let me take it all in. One glance at the covers of every *TV Guide* that Lucy appeared on hanging on the wall around the room and I knew that I had fallen into a Lucy treasure trove. Ostensibly it was a billiards room, but from the dust that had settled on the cue sticks, I was sure nobody had shot pool there in years. The pool table was fully covered with tons of magazines, old scripts and other Lucy/Desi memorabilia. There were autographed pictures to Lucy from old friends like Jimmy Stewart, Buster Keaton, Merv Griffin, Clint Eastwood, and Laurel and Hardy, some standing in frames, others just piled up on shelves next to boxes marked CHRISTMAS 1977 and Lucy porcelain plates. You couldn't take a step without tripping over some Lucy artifact. "Hey Lucy, did you ever think of having a garage sale? You could make a fortune. We could grab unsuspecting tourists from the buses that pass by the house and sell the stuff like you and Ethel did when you had to get rid of five hundred pounds of beef in a hurry!" I ad-libbed, "Pssst, come here. Are you tired of paying through the nose for celebrity memorabilia? Do you want some high quality merchandise at low prices? Then tell you what I'm gonna do!" Lucy chuckled, winked, and told me she would keep it in mind if her career dried up.

Behind the guesthouse was an exercise room with a walking machine, a floor mat for exercising, and a ballet barre that Lucy used for stretching. Onna White, who choreographed Lucy in *Mame*, came over a few times a week to work with her. At nearly seventy Lucy was still remarkably limber and agile. The ballet barre immediately reminded me of the episode when Lucy takes ballet lessons and she gets her legs entwined at the barre. Lucy wiped a tear from her eye as she talked about working on that show with real-life good friend Mary Wickes.

Next to the exercise room and right behind the pool were the pool house and changing rooms. When I walked into the pool house it was love at first sight. Not because of the furnishings which, like in the main house, looked as if they were left over from the fifties. And not again from the yellow and green bogus flowers, which sat in plastic pots on plastic end tables. What was it about fake flowers inside the house that Lucy loved so much? Especially when she had so much of the beautiful real thing blooming throughout her property. No, I fell in love with the dozens of framed photos of Lucy from the movie musical *Mame*, which hung on the back wall. There were publicity stills, rehearsal shots, informal photos—all of Lucy in myriad costumes designed by Theodora Van Ruckle. There was Mame as a blonde, Mame as a brunette, Mame with silver hair—Mame with every color hair but red. Lucy said, at first she was reluctant to hang so many pictures of herself— it wasn't her style. But she was so proud of the work she had done on *Mame* that she still enjoyed looking at the photos six years later. And then Lucy mumbled something under her breath about how she still wasn't over the shellacking she took from the critics who panned both her and the film. The pool house had two backgammon tables almost identical to the others, except these had lime green legs and chair cushions. Lucy wanted two tables for the impromptu backgammon tournaments she would have from time to time and only for very close friends.

We walked arm in arm back in to the main house, where now the smell of something burning was coming from the kitchen. Lucy shrieked, "Jeeesus, the franks!" She was cooking up some hot dogs and beans because she knew I loved them and now all the water had boiled out and the frankfurters were shriveled up and stuck to the bottom of the pot, and the baked beans were now black beans. Any minute I expected her to open the oven door and get pinned down by a mammoth loaf of bread. At that moment, not knowing what to do next, she *was* Lucy Ricardo and I was an audience of one watching life imitating art.

While Lucy fixed me a cold sandwich, she ordered me to take my bags back to the guesthouse. "Don't unpack, just come back, hurry up and eat, so we can play. And don't touch anything in your kitchen, you'll hurt yourself!" I remember that's exactly what she said. I had heard that at 1000 North Roxbury Drive, Gary and the staff had a (secret) nickname for Lucy: Sergeant Morton. She loved to bark orders at everyone. To me she was more like "Mama Morton," the jailhouse warden in the Kander and Ebb musical *Chicago*. And I was Lucy's newest prisoner. I couldn't care less: solitary confinement was going to be just fine with me.

I ate over the kitchen counter. "Milk is good with that kind of sandwich," Lucy said, still scrubbing the burnt franks and beans from the bottom of the pots.

"No, thanks, iced water will be fine."

"Have some milk, *dear!*"

"No thanks, Lucy, I really prefer water, really I do." After I finished my sandwich and drank down my glass of milk like a good boy, we went in to the lanai to play backgammon.

Lucy sat down and immediately lit up a nonfiltered Philip Morris. When Lucy started out in the business she was a model for Chesterfield cigarettes—a Chesterfield Girl, so that's what she smoked. In 1951 she switched to a couple of packs of Philip Morris a day because they were one of the original sponsors of *I Love Lucy*. Like Bill Clinton she claimed she didn't inhale. I loved watching Lucy smoke. The way she held the lighter. The way she cocked her head when she lit the cigarette. The way she *held* the cigarette. The way she pushed the smoke out her mouth. The way she snuffed the cigarette out with one hand while shaking the dice out of the cup with the other. Every little movement seemed to have a meaning all its own.

I loved watching Lucy's hands. They belied her age. They really did. She had hands with long shapely fingers with beautifully manicured nails with the reddest polish I had ever seen.

And they were so expressive, so when Lucy spoke they "spoke" with her. It was quite remarkable. Just watch a *Lucy* episode and watch what she does with her hands. You'll see.

Lucy looked at her watch a lot. It was after two o'clock in the afternoon. "Put some Bobby Darin on the record player, baby," she said. It was sweet how she still called the stereo tape deck a record player. "There are some tapes on top." Lucy loved Bobby Darin and Dean Martin and she listened to them nearly all the time. So we played and listened to *Bobby Darin Live at the Copa*, and Lucy talked about how talented he was and what a shame he died so young. Tears gently ran down her cheeks. Lucy was very sentimental and she prized talent above all else.

There was a small television set on a stand next to the backgammon table, which stayed on but with the sound turned off most of the day. Lucy would raise the volume for daytime game shows like *Password* and *$20,000 Pyramid*. Lucy hated soap operas but she loved word games—playing and watching, at home anyway. Whenever she would appear on *Password*, which she only did because of her close personal relationship with its host, Allen Ludden and his wife, Betty White, she turned into a nervous wreck, literally stuttering away through the show. There are bootlegged videos that have gone around for years of a Lucy guest appearance on *Password* where she appears to be more than slightly inebriated. It was before I spent time with Lucy so I can't positively vouch for her sobriety but knowing her as I did it's incredulous that Lucy would have put herself in such a compromising position on the air. I've looked at the tape and I chalk up her strange behavior to a severe case of "nerves" because when Lucy played games on television she was always so afraid she wouldn't be smart enough for her partner.

Gary came home around four o'clock. Lucy stopped everything, at least for a moment, when Gary came into the room.
She jumped up, gave him a big hug, listened to his funny
stories from the golf course, and laughed out loud. Gary fixed
himself a scotch and water and plunked down in his favorite
club chair, with his feet up on the ottoman. He had a wall
phone right at his side and he called his friend Marvin Davis
to tell him about his day on the links. Gary loved talking to
Marvin and they would call each other at least a half a dozen
times a day.

After talking with Marvin, Gary told Lucy that all the travel
arrangements were made for their upcoming trip to New
York. Little Lucie (that's what friends and family called her to
differentiate her from Big Lucy) was marrying Laurence Luckinbill in June in upstate New York, and Lucy was not looking
forward to the trip. Larry was seventeen years older than Lucie, and that alone made Lucy very unhappy. I couldn't understand Lucy's displeasure, given the fifteen-year age
difference between her and Gary. Who knows, maybe Lucy
thought Gary was older than he really was—he certainly
looked it. The truth was Lucy wasn't crazy about Larry, no
matter how old he was, but I don't think Lucy was ever crazy
about any man her daughter was involved with, let alone planning to marry. Lucy also told me she was very apprehensive
about seeing Desi at the wedding. Now that was something I
totally understood.

We stopped playing backgammon about five o'clock. Lucy
was tired and wanted to go upstairs and rest for a while. She
asked me what time I wanted to eat. I told her six-thirty would
be fine. She said, "We'll have dinner at seven." This way, she
said, we could watch *Wheel of Fortune* and *Jeopardy!* while we ate.
"Then, I think I'll take a little stroll," I said nonchalantly.

"Stroll, what the *hell* are you talking about. You can't stroll in Beverly Hills, it's against the law."

"Lucy, you're funny," I said, but Gary said it was true. He said that you were immediately suspect if you walked around after five o'clock in the evening. He offered me one of his Mercedes, but Lucy immediately revoked the privilege.

"No way, you don't even know where you're going. Take a swim instead and get some late afternoon sun by the pool." Now I knew why she didn't want me to rent a car. Lucy went upstairs and I took a swim. As I jumped into the pool, I had this overwhelming sensation that I was being watched through some closed-circuit camera, which was recording my every move. I couldn't stop laughing. Incarceration was fun.

After my swim I dozed off in the guesthouse and at six-thirty the intercom on my rotary dial guest phone started buzzing like mad. Lucy still had rotary phones—she was one of the biggest creatures of habit I had ever met. She *hated* change, and she was not going to turn in her rotary phones, which were installed back in 1955 when she moved into Roxbury, for those newfangled Touch-Tone ones. Lucy could not even figure out how to use the remote control for her television. Sometimes she got so frustrated with it she threw the damn thing clear across the room. Which reminds me of a time in Palm Springs when Gary bought this humongous television/VCR that was housed in something Lucy thought looked just like a coffin. She hated the thing and made it perfectly clear to Gary. Anyway, with a push of a remote control button the television rose from the top. Another button lowered it. There was a button to push to watch one show and another to push to pop a second show up in the corner of the screen. And there were lots of buttons for the tape deck with A/B switches and all that stuff.

Lucy and I were playing backgammon and when the delivery men were through installing the coffin they handed Lucy the remote control and gave her a blow by blow description of the myriad functions, thinking, of course, that television's "Queen of Comedy" would understand completely. I sat back in my chair, crossed my arms, and savored the moment. Those poor bastards had no idea that *she* had no idea what they were talking about. And I thought, "What a great Lucy episode this could make."

"Where the *hell* are you?" Lucy bellowed into the receiver.

"I thought you said dinner's at seven."

"But we could play for a half hour," she snapped back and hung up. I showered, changed, and was in the house in eight minutes. Lucy was sitting at the table, feverishly shaking the backgammon cup with one hand, checking her watch with the other, and puffing madly on a Philip Morris dangling from her lips. A bourbon and water sat on the end table beside her. "It's about time," she growled. *That* was pure Lucy.

Dinner at the Morton residence was not the formal affair you might think dinner in a Beverly Hills mansion to be. The dress was casual, to say the least. Lucy wore one of her mnemonic monogrammed jogging suits and house slippers. Gary went barefoot in his Brentwood Country Club terry robe. I felt conspicuously overdressed in black chinos and a polo shirt. Lucy sat at the head of the table, her right foot poised on the buzzer buried in the green shag carpet, so she could summon Kum, the chef and Choo, his wife and housekeeper, at will. Gary sat at the other end. I sat to Lucy's left, at the center of the table. Even though it was Thursday and traditionally their day off, Lucy asked Kum to cook dinner that evening in my honor. Personally, I think they heard about Lucy's lunchtime frankfurter fiasco.

The dinner started with a traditional Waldorf salad, which consisted of canned mandarin orange slices and packaged miniature marshmallows. This was one of Lucy's favorite salads. The salad was good, although the marshmallows made me gag. Lucy kept eyeing me with that "You better finish every thing on that plate" look. The main course was veal with vermicelli, which was absolutely delicious and which was Gary's favorite dinner second only to homemade Chinese food. Dessert was a Duncan Hines chocolate cake served with coffee. The three courses were served in exactly one hour, timed precisely to coincide with *Wheel* and *Jeopardy!* Small talk, if any, was confined to commercial breaks. Gary might talk about what was going on at the Lucille Ball Productions office or about a new script he was reading for her. Lucy seemed to care less. And when the show came back on he was cut off in mid-sentence with the snap of her finger.

Lucy loved to play along with the contestants. She was excellent at *Wheel of Fortune*, less successful at *Jeopardy!* Years later on one of my visits to the house, I called up a friend of mine every night in New York and got all the answers to *Wheel of Fortune* and *Jeopardy!*, which had already aired on the East Coast. I sat at dinner with a paper in my lap and "guessed" almost every answer correctly for a week. Lucy was astonished and she told me she was going to call her good friend Merv Griffin, who produced both shows and get me on one of them without even auditioning. Remember when Lucy Ricardo thought Ricky was so smart because he knew all the answers to a radio quiz show, she lined him up as a contestant? When I confessed what I had done Lucy nearly busted a gut laughing. She loved a good joke even when it was on her.

When the game shows were over, we went back into the lanai for some more backgammon. Gary went into his den to call Marvin Davis, and a half-hour later he went upstairs to bed. We played till about ten o'clock. Lucy seemed tired, so I suggested we stop. She kissed me good night and told me not to dare go outside for a walk. "You'll get arrested if you go out," Lucy warned. Arrested, I thought, I'm *already* under house arrest!

I dutifully walked back to the guesthouse through the garden, where the smell of night-blooming jasmine and honeysuckle permeated the evening air. Aqua and magenta lights lit the palms, and the pool shimmered under the moonlight. It was so still except for an occasional car that drove by on the other side of the wall that surrounded the house. I felt safe and serene yet strangely out of place.

I buzzed Lucy on the intercom when I got into the guesthouse and I told her that in the morning I was going to go to the Beverly Hills Hotel for breakfast. I told her rather than asked for her permission. "What the *hell* do you want to go there for?" I said I had never been to the Polo Lounge and I wanted to eat there. "Jeeesus, don't go to the Polo Lounge, it's too damn expensive and the food is God-awful. If you really want to go some place fun go to the Fountain Room, the coffee shop. And look for Thelma—she's there every day at nine. And one more thing *dear*, you better get your ass back here by eleven for backgammon. Now I'm going to bed." Click. "Who's Thelma?" I wondered.

The next morning I went to the Beverly Hills Hotel. I walked down Roxbury Drive one block south to Sunset Boulevard where I turned left and then walked east about a quarter of a mile. I saw nobody on foot except for Japanese gardeners watering the lawns and clipping the hedges in front of some of the most beautiful homes I had ever seen.

The Beverly Hills Hotel was just like it looked in the movies and on picture postcards. Only more pink. I reluctantly but dutifully bypassed the lobby level Polo Lounge, and walked downstairs to the Fountain Room. Why was I going to a coffee shop—to me coffee shops were like Bib and Sam's Luncheonette where I ate breakfast and had egg creams after school when I was growing up in the Bronx. These were the Hills of Beverly—swank. Why couldn't I go to the Polo Lounge if I wanted to? Why did I always have to listen to everything Lucy told me to do? Why was I talking to myself?

As soon as I walked in to the Fountain Room I knew Lucy was right. It had a few tables, and a dozen or so swivel stools at a Formica counter, and it looked like the cover of a *Saturday Evening Post*. Yet at the same time it was very, very chic. There were men at the counter in open-collared Brooks Brothers shirts and khakis reading *Variety*. There were women in wraps over swimsuits with diamonds like doorknobs on their perfectly manicured nails reading *Town and Country*. There were tennis pros from the nearby courts and cabanas. And at the far end of the room on the next to the last stool as the counter curved there was a very well-groomed heavyset woman, busily eating, talking and writing in her Filofax all at the same time.

I asked the waitress with a nametag that read JOHNNIE if there was a Thelma who waited tables. She laughed heartily and pointed to the next to the last stool and said that that was Thelma and the only waiting she was doing was for me. I walked over to Thelma, introduced myself, and asked her if she knew Lucy. She shook my hand with a grip like a vice and said, "Only about forty-five years, that's all, honey. Now c'mon kid, sit down and I'll buy you some breakfast. Johnnie, give him some scrambled and bacon with a bialy shmear, orange juice and coffee, and put it on my tab."

Thelma Orloff was absolutely fascinating. She was about

five feet ten inches tall with perfectly coifed silver-gray hair. She was about the same age as Lucy, seventy, but to me looked some years younger. And although she was probably well over two hundred pounds, her weight seemed to complement the smartness of her dress rather than detract from it. Thelma Orloff met Lucille Ball in the middle of the 1930s when they were in their twenties and were both under contract to RKO. Thelma had bit parts in films, among them a movie Lucy costarred in called *Having Wonderful Time*. In those "Golden Days of Hollywood" Thelma was known as a *glamazon*—a big, shapely, full-bodied beauty whose presence could fill a screen even in a walk-on. She reached into her satchel of a pocketbook filled with Mark Cross leather everything and pulled out a nearly fifty-year-old snapshot of her taken by the studio to prove it.

After Thelma left the business she went into real estate, and was now working for Stan Herman selling multimillion-dollar homes in Beverly Hills, Holmby Hills, and Bel-Air, the superrich area known as "The Golden Triangle." Thelma was hugely successful at selling homes around town where she earned the nickname "Realty Royalty." Thelma was married to screenwriter Arthur Orloff, who was now retired and in frail health. They had a daughter named Kathy who worked in film. And for the last twenty-five years, every Monday through Thursday between eight-thirty and nine-thirty in the morning Thelma Orloff held court on the next to the last stool in the Fountain Room of the Beverly Hills Hotel. On Fridays she arrived a half-hour later because she got her hair done in the hotel's beauty salon. What immediately intrigued me about Thelma Orloff was her self-assuredness, yet without a trace of braggadocio.

The bacon and scrambled eggs at the Fountain Room were

the best I had ever tasted. It was like eating breakfast from Phipps Department Store's Fountain and Tea Room when Lucy Ricardo says, "Food from Phipps always tastes different, I don't know *what* they did to it." Or maybe the food was so good because while I was eating Thelma Orloff was regaling me with stories about making movies in the thirties and selling real estate in the eighties. In one breath she would tell me about palling around with Cary Grant and Randolph Scott in the hills above Hollywood (I'll bet she knew who was sleeping with whom in those days). And in another, she would tell me about "teardowns"—homes that people were buying for outrageous sums of money and completely demolishing only to rebuild on the same lot. She told me about a small property she was just about to close on but the buyers were hesitant because there was no place to swim. "I told them, it's only a million three, all you have to do is drop in a pool for another hundred thou or so." Drop in a pool—that was the coolest real estate expression I had ever heard.

Thelma's stories were so wonderful I completely lost track of time. Thelma didn't. She told me she had to get me back to the house by eleven. Lucy covered all her bases. Thelma looked like my parole officer or something as she escorted me back upstairs and out to the hotel driveway where her black Cadillac sedan with ORLOFF plates was waiting for us. We went back through Benedict Canyon Drive up to Lexington, made a left, and came down and made a right on to Roxbury. She dropped me at the curb and I thanked her for a great breakfast and conversation and told her I hoped I would see her again soon. "You will, honey," she said, "I'll be over at three for backgammon." I looked at my watch: ten-fifty seven. Whew, made it!

I walked into the lanai and there was Lucy at the backgammon table watching something on television. She looked at her watch. "It's five after eleven. Now, sit down and play and tell me all about breakfast with fatso." That was Lucy's term of endearment for Thelma behind her back. I told Lucy how taken I was with Thelma and her stories. "Wait till fatso sits down and plays backgammon with you. A couple of games with her and you'll run for the pool. Now enough about Thelma, turn down the set and let's play, and I hope you got going-out out of your system."

"Yes, sir!" With that Lucy rolled the dice.

As promised, Thelma pulled into the driveway at precisely three o'clock and rang the side doorbell. "Jeeesus, Dr. Jeckyl is here. You better get your bathing suit on," Lucy warned me. Thelma's high-heeled pumps clicked loudly across the parquet foyer floor, and then the noise subsided when they hit the shag rug in the lanai. I got up to greet her as she walked into the room. Lucy kept her head down as if she was deeply engrossed in her game even though it was my roll. "Hey, red, how's your FS?" Thelma asked.

"What's an FS?" I asked. Lucy's FS was her "fucking shoulder," the left one which was afflicted with bursitis, and which kept her from having anywhere near a full range of motion.

"Get me some iced tea honey, one Sweet'n Low, and make sure it's cold," Thelma asked/ordered.

We played chouettes for the rest of the afternoon. Thelma was losing a few dollars, not much, but she was not happy. The more she lost the harder she rolled the dice. Sometimes they would roll off the table and Lucy would mutter some curse words to herself as I scampered around in the shag retrieving the dice. Thelma would also hover over the table, leaning heavily on it with both arms. At times the table would actually tilt, which made Lucy nuts. At five o'clock Gary came home and gave Thelma hell about parking her car in the driveway so he couldn't get his car into the garage. From his tone and her casual response I gathered that Thelma had done this before. "Here, take my keys honey and move my car onto the street," Thelma told me. And the next thing I knew I was backing Gary's Rolls out of the driveway, then Thelma's Cadillac on to the street, then Gary's Rolls into the garage. I felt like a valet parking attendant.

We played until about six o'clock. Lucy was winning but I could sense she was getting tired and restless. Thelma was losing and angry. Lucy was right, I did want to go for a swim. We settled up. Thelma threw her money on the table, said a quick good-bye and was out of there. Lucy immediately gave me one of those didn't-I-tell-you-so looks and then took a nap with Tinker in her arms on the divan in the lanai. At seven, Gary, Lucy, and I had a quiet dinner with Vanna White and Alex Trebeck, and then Lucy and I played backgammon while Gary spoke on the phone with his buddies.

The next day was Saturday and Lucy strongly suggested that I have breakfast in the house and relax. Relax, if I was any more relaxed, I'd be dead. I took her suggestion and the next morning Kum fixed me a delicious breakfast. I then went into the living room and took one of the leather-bound books with original scripts marked I Love Lucy and brought it back to the den where I found the corresponding videotape and watched episode after episode following along with the script. I was fascinated by the pencil annotations in the margins, which indicated script changes. I assumed they were Lucy's. All of a sudden it felt like I wasn't alone. I turned and Lucy was standing in the doorway watching Lucy with me. It was very strange. I remember the show. The Ricardos and the Mertzs were visiting Ethel's hometown of Albuquerque on their way out to California where Ricky was going to star in *Don Juan*. Ethel was bragging to her father about her life in show business pretending she was the star of the film. It's a classic episode, like all 179 of them.

"God, wasn't Viv brilliant," Lucy said. "She played everything with such truth." When I told Lucy that she was pretty funny, too, she told me to shut up and watch Vivian Vance if I wanted to learn about comedy. I turned back to the set. Lucy left in tears.

We played backgammon all weekend and I watched Lucy whenever I wasn't watching Lucy. Monday was Memorial Day and Lucy decided to have a backgammon tournament and barbecue. She invited Gary's sister, Helen, Thelma Orloff, and Pat and Charlie Stone, who were close friends of Lucy and Gary. Also invited was Jeanine Forman, who was the widow of comedian Joey Forman who Gary knew from his days doing stand-up in the borscht belt. Gary hated backgammon, but was actually quite good and he begrudgingly agreed to play if Lucy let him play golf, so the tournament began at five o'clock.

It was a very fun night. We played in the pool house and stopped just long enough to eat hamburgers and hot dogs expertly prepared by Kum on the outdoor grill. The beverage of choice, Lucy's choice, was ice water. When I asked for red wine with dinner Lucy just made believe she didn't hear me. And what a shame, because Lucy and Gary had a closet full of marvelous wines and champagnes, which rarely, if ever, were opened. After dinner we went right back to the tournament. Thelma was in a great mood all evening—she was winning.

I was supposed to go home on Tuesday, but when I was packing Lucy started to cry and I couldn't take it so I stayed on another few days. Lucy turned on the "water works" with those baby blues real fast to get what she wanted—a trait she surely inherited from her alter ego Lucy Ricardo. Anyway, it worked and I stayed until the end of the week. We played lots of backgammon, ate lots of Waldorf salads, watched *Wheel of Fortune* and *Jeopardy!*, and I only left the house to meet Thelma for breakfast every weekday morning.

I met just one other celebrity that week; one morning I was walking home from the Beverly Hills Hotel and I literally bumped into Peter Falk as I turned the corner onto Roxbury Drive. I told him I was a big fan and that he was the first famous person I had actually seen in Beverly Hills. When he asked where I was staying and I told him, he gave me a Columbo sort of look and walked off.

Lucy's Back in Town

IN JUNE LUCY AND GARY FLEW BACK east for Lucie and Larry's wedding in upstate New York. So did Desi Arnaz and his redheaded wife, Edie. At the time I was not at all close to Lucie and so I was not invited to the wedding. Lucy called to say what a wonderful day it was. Lucie and Larry were married in an apple orchard among family and close friends. Desi serenaded mother and daughter with the theme from *Forever Darling*, an MGM film that Lucy and Desi made in 1955. Lucy was choked up just talking to me about it.

Lucy went right back to Los Angeles and never made it back to Manhattan that summer. Gary hated New York, especially in the heat, and Lucy did not feel comfortable flying alone. But we spoke lots on the phone and she promised to make a trip back east when the weather got cold. As Jamestown, New York's favorite "daughter," Lucy loved the change of seasons, especially winter, especially snow. So the next January she came back for a visit. And she came alone. Doing my best Lucy imitation over the phone I ordered, "Don't check any luggage, just carry it on. This way you can get out of the airport faster and get right to the hotel so we can play lots of backgammon." Lucy knew I was putting her on, so she just hung up.

Ambrose and I met Lucy at the airport. At that time airport security was not what it is today, and I met her on the plane as soon as it arrived at the gate. She was sitting at a window seat in the last row of first class. She looked sensational. She was wearing a chocolate brown skirt and a paisley blouse. Over the blouse she wore a sable vest. When I approached her, I pretended to be a flight attendant and asked her if she had a good trip. Lucy was peering into her makeup mirror, applying gobs of red lipstick while fussing with her hair, and straightening her neckerchief. She looked up to thank me, and shrieked, "What the hell are you doing here?" Scaring the hell out of everybody around her.

We met Ambrose at baggage claim where three of her eight matching monogrammed L.B.M. pieces had already come off the conveyor belt. Lucy traveled like a star. A big star. All told, there were two steamer trunks, three suitcases, two hanging garment bags, and an overnight case. This did not include a forty-five-pound tote bag, which I schlepped from the plane that was loaded with books, make-up, two plastic bags full of medication, and a portable backgammon set. "With all this luggage, are you back here for a vacation or to make a movie?"

"If only anybody wanted me," Lucy whispered in my ear.

Lucy checked into the same suite at the Helmsley Palace that she had the year before. The moment she stepped in the room she said, "I need a backgammon fix." So she quickly unpacked all her bags, which were filled with scads of pants suits, skirts and tops, fur coats, and the obligatory jogging suits which, except when she went on interviews, was all she wore the last time she was in town. We played backgammon until midnight and then Lucy said, "I'll see you tomorrow, baby, around noon, and I *mean* noon!" Lucy never realized I had to work for a living. Or if she did she didn't care.

Lucy was in town to do a weeklong series of interviews with David Hartman on *Good Morning America,* which she was going to tape in one session. So she was going to have plenty of time on those gorgeous hands of hers, which needed constant holding when she wasn't working. Of course, I wanted to be with Lucy, as did Tom, so we took turns taking off from work in the afternoon to play backgammon. We both spent all our evenings with Lucy. We made a pact with her: We would stay in the suite by day, but at night, I told Lucy, "We're going to paint the town *red!*"

She loved the pun and hated the idea. "No way!" she countered. "I don't like going to restaurants and I hate the theater." "No way" was one of Lucy's favorite expressions whenever anybody suggested doing anything that required leaving the house or taking off her jogging suit. I knew Lucy loved all that Manhattan had to offer. But she was just so used to saying, "No." She was also terrified of crowds, being for the last few years so isolated in Beverly Hills, where she hardly socialized outside her home. I assured her that Tom and I and three hundred-plus-pound Ambrose would be able to come between her and anybody. Lucy reluctantly agreed to one night out—dinner and a show, but one night only.

The one night only turned into scores of nights on the town—Broadway openings, concerts, movies, nightclubs, and restaurants—with Lucy always on my arm. Lucy could not get enough of New York. It was as if she had just stepped off the bus from Jamestown like she had done for the first time when she was sixteen. Lucy came back as often as she could, sometimes with Gary, sometimes alone. And even when Gary was in town, he would rarely go to dinner with us. And he hated the theatre. So most nights he would dine with Lew Rudin and his other cronies, downtown at Sammy's Roumanian, or uptown at Elaine's. Meanwhile Lucy and I saw just about every Broadway and Off-Broadway musical there was to see. It was great fun taking Lucy backstage after the show to meet with the casts or watching people do triple-takes in the neighborhood restaurants we frequented uptown and down.

Lucy grew tired of the Palace and decided she wanted a smaller hotel, nearer "The Boys" as she always referred to Tom and me. We lived on Park Avenue and Eighty-first Street, so she decided on the Hotel Westbury at Sixty-ninth Street and Madison Avenue. The Westbury, now a condominium apartment building, was at the time one of Manhattan's most chic, boutique hotels. Lucy took an elegant, two-bedroom suite, and unlike the Helmsley Palace, which had hundreds of rooms, the Westbury had less than eighty. Lucy was always treated like Hollywood royalty.

Soon Lucy grew tired of hotel living altogether so she and Gary decided to take an apartment in one of Lew Rudin's rental buildings. In 1983 Lucie and Larry and their four kids (two from Larry's first marriage to actress Robin Strasser, and two of their own) were also living in Manhattan. Lucy and Gary moved into a two-bedroom, two-bathroom apartment on the twenty-sixth floor of a postwar doorman building at 211 East Seventieth Street. They enjoyed a fabulous East River view and their neighbors in the building included Lena Horne, Kaye Ballard, Virginia Graham, and lyricist Carolyn Leigh, who had written the lyrics to *Wildcat*. The rent was $2,500 a month, which Lucy thought was exorbitant. (Actually at the time it was slightly below market price for an apartment of its size. Today that same apartment would rent for well over $6,000 a month.)

When Lucy told me about the place, I told her, "We could visit the Ricardos and the Mertzs, who live a few blocks away at 623 East Sixty-eighth Street." An address that in reality would have placed them somewhere in the middle of New York's East River.

"How the hell do you remember the address?" Lucy asked, incredulously.

I snapped back, "If you watched the show more often instead of playing backgammon all day, you'd know it, too!" We both laughed out loud.

Lucy was as excited as a new bride moving into her first apartment. She called her friend Paula Stewart who was living in Los Angeles to come east and help decorate the place. Paula Stewart, after a short-lived marriage to composer Burt Bachrach, had married and divorced Jack Carter. Paula left show business and was now dabbling in real estate on the West Coast as well as doing some interior design work. Her most famous client was Ruth Pointer, of the Pointer Sisters, for whom she had done a couple of homes in Beverly Hills and Las Vegas. Paula jumped at the opportunity to do Lucy's apartment, and being resourceful, managed to get herself a studio apartment at 211 East Seventieth Street.

Lucy basically needed everything for the new apartment except stainless steel flatware. Because once she knew she was moving, Lucy began to systematically steal (she liked to say borrow) a few pieces of silverware every day from room service deliveries, and soon she had service for eight with the unwitting compliments of the Hotel Westbury. Let me back up for a moment. You see Lucy realized that the *W* for Westbury engraved on the knives, forks, and spoons turned into an M for Morton when you turned them around. So with the help of "The Boys," who took silverware home in their pockets each night, Lucy appropriated a lovely set of dining utensils. I suggested to Tom that while we were at it, we should take some for ourselves—perfect for his last name, Wells—but, alas, he didn't agree. Lucy even managed to appropriate seventeen serving pieces to her newfound loot.

The only snafu to the silverware caper happened when Lucy was checking out of the hotel for the very last time. In the elevator, the bellboy accidentally overturned her tote bag, and out flew five soupspoons, seven salad forks, and a butter knife. Lucy didn't flinch—she stared straight up at the numbers, as I (on my hands and knees) quickly retrieved the stainless "steal" and put it back in the bag. By the time we reached the lobby, it was as if nothing happened. The staff thanked Lucy profusely for her loyal patronage, and after she signed some autographs for the doormen and bell captains, they applauded wildly as she left the hotel. As we drove off to Lucy's new digs I thought, Here was another incident where life imitated art—it was the Lucy "The Kleptomaniac" episode all over again and almost as funny.

Paula filled Lucy's days busily running her from one interior design showroom to another picking things for the apartment. Lucy was much too much a control freak to give Paula creative or financial carte blanche when it came to furnishing her home, so she went everywhere with Paula even though she cursed Paula everyday for spending so much time and money on the place. Of course there were no prices on anything they bought since everything was in designer showrooms. One day I tagged along with Lucy and Paula, and I watched Lucy trying to inconspicuously look for the price tag on a sofa she liked, figuring maybe it was hidden somewhere in the fabric. Again, sound familiar? Like when Lucy Ricardo goes shopping with Betty Ramsey to furnish her new home in Westport.

When the apartment was finished I was surprised at the look of Lucy's new place. Unlike her Beverly Hills home, this had a more formal look; the L-shaped living room had bergere chairs done with cream color ultra-suede seats, a French Provincial backgammon table with fruit wood chairs and mauve cushions, and beige wall-to-wall plush velvet carpet. There was a huge glass etagere on one wall, which held Lucy's Emmy Awards and artfully framed family photos. The dining room had a formal mahogany dining table with eight chairs. One thing though that I thought was hysterical—Paula had copies of Monets, Matisses, and Renoirs done by an artist friend in Beverly Hills and they were hung all over the apartment. This puzzled our banker friend Alec who, when he came by to open some New York bank accounts for Lucy and Gary, could not understand why the paint on the *Water Lilies* was still wet.

Apart from the second bedroom, which was turned into Gary's den and multimedia room, and which was furnished beautifully yet comfortably, everything about the rest of the apartment was very done and very beige. Not like Lucy's other homes at all. I soon discovered both Paula and Lucy each had "interior" motives for what they had created.

Paula was dying to get Lucy's new Manhattan apartment photographed by *Architectural Digest* and she did. She made sure the photographer didn't get too close to the damp paintings. I still can't believe *AD* did not see through the fakes. Who knows? Maybe they did. But it didn't matter because the banner headline across the cover of the magazine touted Lucille Ball's new Manhattan apartment with a five-page spread inside.

As for Lucy, she said she loved being near her new grandchildren, yet she seemed very nervous whenever they were around her. So the formality of the apartment "told" everybody that the kids would not be welcome there and if Lucy wanted to visit them, she would go to Lucie's apartment on the upper West Side. Which is exactly what she did, though not very often. It was sad, because it seemed to me like it was always such an obligation for Lucy to be with her children and now with her grandchildren as well.

Lucie had a great big prewar apartment on Central Park West and Eighty-seventh Street, with high ceilings and which was furnished with an eclectic mix of very expensive antiques next to pieces picked up at flea markets. Lucie had a great sense of style and it was always reflected in her homes and in her dress. It was accompanying Lucy on one of her infrequent outings to Lucie's apartment on Central Park West that she spoke one of her most classic bon mots. We were riding in the limousine one evening heading west through the Central Park Transverse and Lucy was gazing out of the window into the darkened night. "I hate the Upper West Side," she said.

I couldn't resist challenging Lucy—I never could—so I countered with, "How can you make such a blanket statement like that?"

"Because, I just did, that's how," Lucy answered back.

I took a different tack. "Lucy, then what *is* it about the Upper West Side that you hate?"

She thought for a few moments, and without turning her head, which was pressed against the window said, "It's so, it's so . . . it's so Lauren Bacall!!" There was nothing more to say.

EPISODE SIX

Lucy & Miracles

WHILE LUCY WAS SPENDING MORE
and more time in Manhattan, I was spending more and more
time trying to figure out a way to keep her in town even
longer. Visiting for a couple of weeks at a time four or five
times a year wasn't enough for me. When Lucy was with Gary
in the winter he was eager to get back to Beverly Hills where
he could play golf. When Lucy traveled alone, she said she
missed her toy poodle, Tinker, who never traveled with her.
I knew only work would keep Lucy in New York for an extended stay, but nobody was offering her any scripts she liked
enough to do on either coast.

I took Lucy to see *Steel Magnolias* and *Driving Miss Daisy*, two
big Off-Broadway hits in the 1980s. Lucy loved them both
and was particularly drawn to the character of Miss Daisy herself—a feisty, cantankerous, old Southern widow living in At-
lanta, whose son, despite her protestations, hires a black
chauffeur to drive her around town. Lucy talked about that
play for weeks after we saw it and I knew she wanted to play
Miss Daisy if and when the film was made. As much as I
wanted to see Lucy work, I thought she was all wrong for the
part. Lucy's fans wanted to see *Lucy* the scatterbrain, the mis-
chief maker, the clown. Daisy, for the most part was not a

likeable character, and it was impossible not to love Lucy. Gary campaigned hard for Lucy to do the movie but ultimately, the part went to Jessica Tandy, who won an Oscar for best actress and the movie won an Oscar for best picture the year after Lucy died.

Lucy's stereotype was both a blessing and a curse. In one of our first conversations about the business, Lucy told me she could not understand actors who said they resented being typecast. She said that she always wanted to find that niche, that instant recognition from an audience for a character that was hers and hers alone. She had never found it in the close to seventy films she had made, except for critics recognizing her as "The Queen of the B's."

So in 1951, the year Lucie Arnaz was born in real life and Lucy Ricardo was "born" on the small screen, Lucille Ball was ecstatic about creating a television persona that in one incarnation or another, would endure for the next twenty-five years and make her legendary. The blessing itself turned into a curse when Lucy, now in her seventies, found herself looking for roles that would complement the beloved character she created. With Vivian Vance and William Frawley gone and Desi now in retirement and in failing health, Lucy knew how difficult it would be to do another series. "We could never top what we had and I wouldn't even want to try," Lucy, in interviews, had said countless times.

I said to Tom, "Why doesn't Lucy do a Broadway show?" Although *Wildcat* was a critical and ultimately commercial failure, the audiences loved it. Lucy's ill health and exhaustion closed the show, not the reviews. Even the musical film version of *Mame*, which critics slaughtered, broke box office records at Radio City Music Hall. But could Lucy do eight shows a week? If she collapsed on stage twenty years ago, could she sustain herself now? And then there was the challenge of finding the right vehicle to show Lucy off at her best.

Max Allentuck, the late Broadway general manager who once was married to Maureen Stapleton, and Steve Martin, who directed Broadway show commercials, had obtained the theatrical option to Frank Capra's 1961 film *Pocketful of Miracles*, which starred Bette Davis and Glenn Ford. Based on a short story by Damon Runyon, *Pocketful of Miracles* was a heartwarming tale of Apple Annie, a beggar who hung out on Broadway with a basket of apples and sold them to among others, bootlegger Dave the Dude, who thinks her apples bring him luck. Meanwhile Annie has a daughter living in a convent in Spain whom she regularly writes to and tells that she is a part of New York's high society. When her daughter writes back to say she is coming to New York so her mother can meet her fiancé, a count, Annie is in a jam. She turns to Dave the Dude, his girlfriend Queenie and the rest of his Runyonesque pals to turn her into a lady for a day and convince the count that he is hobnobbing with New York's elite.

One night over drinks at Sardi's, Max, Steve, Tom, and I convinced one another that Lucy would be perfect as Apple Annie. They shared my concerns about Lucy's ability to carry a show eight times a week, but the role was tailor-made for Lucy and it was too good an opportunity to pass up. Now all we had to do was convince Lucy. We anticipated no trouble raising the money to produce the show, which in 1982 would have been around two million dollars. Our plan was for Lucy to open the show, do the first six months, and then we would replace her. We knew that one full-page ad in the Sunday *New York Times* heralding Lucy's return to Broadway in a new musical would sell out the house for her whole six-month run. Now all we had to do was convince Lucy.

I was confident Lucy would be intrigued by *Miracles*, if nothing else because the part of a bag lady meant she wouldn't have to worry about the way she looked on stage. Lucy was incredibly vain and very self-conscious about her appearance in public. She was deathly afraid of cosmetic surgery and never had a face-lift, so whenever she worked she wore wigs where the facial skin was pulled up and tucked under netting attached to the hair. It was quite uncomfortable but she would not appear on camera any other way. I always thought Lucy looked better and *younger* when she went out with her own hair, a scarf around her neck, and wearing those big, tinted eyeglasses.

One night over dinner, I mentioned *Miracles* to Lucy, and she stopped me in mid-sentence and said, "No way," which in no way surprised me. Right then and there I deliberately dropped the subject, and she dropped her jaw when I so easily took no for an answer. We frequently bantered back and forth over things, so Lucy was surprised when I gave up so easily. Getting Lucy to agree to even be receptive to the idea of doing *Miracles* had to be carefully finessed, so I told Lucy that she was absolutely right, it was a ridiculous idea, what was I thinking? Later that evening, back in her apartment while we were playing backgammon, out of the blue, with her blue eyes glued to the board, Lucy mumbled under her breath just loud enough for me to hear, "What the *hell* do I want to do a Broadway musical for? I can't sing, I can't dance anymore, *Jeeesus*, are you crazy or something?" Hmmm, Lucy was interested.

A few weeks later when Lucy was back on the coast, she called me and asked about *Miracles*. Who were we planning to cast and was I still involved? I told her I really had no interest in the project if she had no interest in it, and that I believed Max and Steve were talking to among others Maureen Stapleton and Angela Lansbury. Lucy interrupted, "I never said I wasn't *interested*, I just said I couldn't sing or dance."

"Oh," I said.

Lucy continued, "Is there any music written yet? Maybe you could get Cy Coleman to do the score?" Lucy loved Cy Coleman, who along with Carolyn Leigh had written the score for *Wildcat*. "Yeah, maybe," I said again. "Lucy, what else is new?" I asked matter-of-factly.

"What kind of producer are you anyway," Lucy inquired in her inimitable style and then she hung up. Hmmm, Lucy was very interested.

Wally Harper has been Barbara Cook's musical director and arranger for over twenty-five years. He has also done dance arrangements, been the conductor and musical supervisor for many Broadway shows, and wrote additional songs for the Broadway revival of *Irene*, and the dance music for the film *The Best Little Whorehouse in Texas*. In early 1983, Steve Martin approached Wally about writing a few songs for *Miracles* specifically for Lucy. With Lucy's vocal range, it would be a challenge.

Wally asked David Zippel to write the lyrics. David was writing Off-Broadway revues and collaborating with Wally Harper on special material for Barbara Cook. By the end of the decade David would win a Tony Award for *City of Angels*, collaborating with Cy Coleman, and in the 1990s write the lyrics for two Disney films, *Hercules* and *Mulan*. Although now we are the best of friends, at that time I had never met "Zip."

There was trouble in Beverly Hills. As Lucy grew more interested in and enthused about *Miracles*, Gary became more disenchanted. He despised New York and the possibility of living there with Lucy for close to a year made him crazy. If it wasn't for his pal Lew Rudin, Gary would have had no interest at all in coming east. Gary however was *always* interested in how much money Lucy made. And no matter what Lucy would make doing *Miracles*, it was nowhere near the amount of money she could command for a television movie of the week or feature film. So for Gary, *Miracles* was a no-win situation.

Wally and David wrote five songs for *Miracles*. Lucy flew to New York, listened to them and liked what she heard. She now was very excited about the prospect of a return to Broadway. But things on the producing end were moving slowly. Jimmy Nederlander, head of the Nederlander Organization, the second largest producer of Broadway shows, who along with Max and Steve held the option to *Miracles*, was reluctant to invest in Lucy. She was no doubt a huge box office draw, but the Nederlander's remembered Lucy's exhaustion and collapse during the run of *Wildcat*, and had trepidation about backing Lucy even for a limited run. Without their financial support it would be almost impossible to produce the show. Lucy was of course unaware of the dilemma, and after talking about *Miracles* for over a year Lucy was now hoping it would come true.

Miracles, unfortunately, never got produced on Broadway, with or without Lucy. The option ran out and subsequent legal battles over who owns the rights—MGM, which produced the movie or the Damon Runyon estate—to this day keep the project grounded.

Lucy became so obsessed with the notion of playing a bag lady that in 1985 she signed on to do a television movie called *Stone Pillow* about a homeless woman living on the streets of Manhattan. Unlike the comedic *Pocketful of Miracles*, *Stone Pillow* was a somber story, and neither the critics nor the TV audience appreciated Lucy playing so against type. The screenplay was weak and Lucy was just plain not believable in the role. Filmed on location in Manhattan during a particularly hot summer, Lucy collapsed from exhaustion and dehydration toward the end of the shoot, which brought on a host of other ailments that plagued her for the rest of her life.

If there was ever a time Lucy and I needed to be with each other it was during the *Stone Pillow* shoot—to help her learn her lines, to keep her company between takes, to have dinner and play backgammon every night together. Unfortunately, and not by choice, I was nowhere near. A few months earlier Lucy decided that she never wanted to see me again.

Lucy & Me (Not)

MY CLOSE FRIENDSHIP WITH LUCY came to a screeching halt in Ambrose's limousine in late October 1984. An altercation that lasted only a few minutes provoked an estrangement that lasted over a year. I remember that day very well because the night before Lucy had fainted in my arms. We were in her New York apartment, just the two of us playing backgammon. Every half-hour or so Lucy reached into her purse and took out some sort of smelling salts (to me it looked like amyl nitrate "poppers"), broke one open, and took a big whiff. "Lucy, why are you doing that? I asked. "They help me breathe easier," she said. About ten o'clock, while we were playing, Lucy began to perspire, hyperventilate, and grow very pale. I suggested we stop and when she readily agreed in the middle of a game, I knew something was wrong. As she got up from the table, her legs buckled under, and she collapsed in my arms.

I immediately called 911 and the paramedics were there within five minutes. Before they arrived Lucy regained consciousness. I picked her up from the living room carpet and carried her into bed. It was like the end of *The Big Street* when Henry Fonda carried Lucy up that fabulous sweeping stairway. Except now Lucy wore a tattered, terry cloth robe and bunny slippers instead of high heels and a ball gown. "What the hell are you doing?" Lucy asked as she came to in a state of confusion.

"A remake of *The Big Street*, your highness, and I don't mind telling you, you weigh a ton!" Lucy sighed.

Two paramedics came and went into her bedroom, and after fifteen minutes or so they came out with a couple of autographs and told me Lucy was going to be fine. "God," I wondered, "Would Lucy one day be signing autographs on her deathbed?" Lucy had told them about some of the medication she was taking but not about the "poppers." They seemed more interested in looking at her Emmy Awards displayed on the glass etagere in the living room than in discussing her health. They said Lucy should not be left alone. Gary was in California and Paula was out for the evening so, of course, I stayed with Lucy.

I called Gary in Beverly Hills, who did not seem overly concerned about Lucy's condition. He said he was not aware of any heart medication Lucy was taking. And then he told me that he was going out to dinner with Marvin Davis and that he would call me when he got back. Then he hung up.

I slept on the divan in the living room, tossing and turning and tiptoeing every so often into Lucy's room to make sure she was sleeping soundly. She awoke about ten the next morning and said she felt fine and I could tell she was very embarrassed over what had happened the night before. "Let's go out for dinner tonight. Someplace fun, just the two of us, you name it, baby," Lucy said, hugging me for dear life.

"You should faint more often," I said.

Lucy never wanted to go out for dinner so I knew she was grateful. "But you know Lee Tannen, you look like hell so go home and get some sleep."

When Lucy hired Paula to do her Manhattan apartment, Paula decided to move back to New York permanently. It was the summer of 1983 and Tom and I were spending it on Corfu, Greece, having got fed up with our jobs at the advertising agency. Paula and her teenage son moved into our place while we were gone. She wanted to spend time in New York looking for things for Lucy's apartment, and we felt good about someone keeping an eye on our apartment. When we returned from Europe we found that Paula had done her own bit of redecorating to our place, rehanging pictures, moving furniture, adding some of her own. Nothing major, just enough to be disconcerting to someone like myself who likes everything in its proper place, and is not crazy about any kind of change. Paula apologized and moved out and we moved things back where they belonged.

We had a fairly large apartment on Park Avenue and Paula asked if she could leave a few things there since she was anticipating an imminent move back east. I agreed, and we gave her a closet in the guest bedroom for the stuff she left behind. Paula returned to her home in Coldwater Canyon. A few weeks later she called and asked us if she could ship a few more cartons back to our apartment, until the studio apartment which she had rented in Lucy's building was ready. She gave us the date that the boxes would arrive.

A couple of weeks later at five o'clock one afternoon, a Mayflower moving van, about as long as one city block pulled up in front of our building. Earlier in the day, we had alerted our building manager that we were expecting a delivery, and if necessary to keep the freight elevator open for a few minutes longer than usual. When the doorman buzzed us and suggested we come down to see just what was being delivered I knew something was up. I got to the lobby and saw four men unloading over a hundred boxes off the truck. Boxes that contained everything from clothes, books, paintings, pots and pans—even three Oriental rugs. It took four hours to get everything into our apartment and her "odds and ends" took up a fifteen by twenty-foot guestroom and almost half of our bedroom.

Our neighbors thought someone new had moved in. I was flabbergasted and didn't know what to think. I called Paula in Los Angeles and she said she didn't think she had *that* many boxes until the movers came to pack, and then it was too late. "But don't worry honey," she said, "I'll have everything out within the month." Which month, Paula? I thought.

Lucy moved into her two-bedroom apartment, and Paula moved into her studio shortly thereafter. Unfortunately nothing moved from ours. Whenever I mentioned getting the boxes out, Paula made some excuse about having to get them into storage, since there was no room in her small apartment. Whenever I talked to Lucy about it she defended Paula, saying how unhappy she was, how she had no money, how I had to be more patient with her. As the weeks passed, I instead got more and more pissed off.

Paula was now firmly ensconced in New York and on Lucy's payroll. And she was at Lucy's beck and call. Lucy was almost fanatically loyal and devoted to Paula, and I never understood why. Maybe it was because Paula introduced her to Gary. Maybe she just felt sorry for her, I don't know. Anyway, most evenings the four of us, Paula, Tom, Lucy, and I had dinner together and then went back to Lucy's apartment to play backgammon. Paula was not as enamored of the game as we were so she would leave early for a date or just go back down to her apartment, which suited me fine.

One day in late October, the day after Lucy fainted in my

arms and six months after our apartment turned into Manhattan Mini-Storage, Tom was moving around some of the
heavier boxes when his back went out. He was in excruciat-
ing pain, and I didn't want to leave Tom alone and go out
but I didn't want to break my date and disappoint Lucy, so I
went. After all, I had saved Lucy's life. At least, that's what
she told everybody she spoke to on the phone the next day
on the West Coast. Besides Paula was busy that evening, so it
was just going to be Lucy and me.

When Lucy called late in the afternoon to make dinner plans
I told her what happened to Tom, and how it happened. She
knew I was upset, as I don't hide those things well. But she
didn't say a word or even try to apologize for Paula. Ambrose
picked me up in front of my apartment building at seven
o'clock, and when I got in Paula was in the backseat. I couldn't
believe it. How could Lucy have asked her knowing how I
felt? Paula said she heard what happened to Tom, and then
Lucy said how sorry Paula was. Uncharacteristically, I didn't
say a word.

We went to dinner at Billy's, a steakhouse on First Avenue
and Fifty-second Street. I was very quiet all through dinner.
Lucy tried making jokes and Paula tried making up. But I was
still seething and just wanted to go home. I said I had a bad
headache and begged off playing backgammon at Lucy's. I
knew Lucy would be disappointed and I didn't care. On the
way back to my place, frustrated by my unusually quiet demeanor, Lucy said something like "I don't understand why
you're so upset, can't you see how badly Paula feels?"

I went ballistic. "You don't understand why I'm so upset?
All right Lucy," I condescendingly said, "I'll try to explain it
to you. I'll bring a hundred boxes over to your apartment and
see how you like it. You go crazy if the slightest thing is out

of place and you practically have an anxiety attack whenever Lucie brings your grandson over to play!" I went on and on. I was so mad, I was like a crazy person, and I was scaring the hell out of Lucy, Paula, even Ambrose, who kept staring at me through the rearview mirror. Lucy froze and Paula grabbed hold of her arm and on cue started to cry. Then my tantrum was over, and I was so sorry I had lost my temper.

Lucy immediately instructed Ambrose to turn the car around and take her home. She was stuttering badly and biting down hard on her lip, something she did only when she got very angry or upset. Meanwhile I started apologizing profusely but nobody said anything. When we pulled into Lucy's driveway Paula got out first but Lucy stayed in her seat. She took off her dark glasses and her eyes were all bloodshot. Then she just stared at me. In a few seconds she got out and as she slammed the door in my face I lowered the window and said, "Good-night, Lucy, I'll see you tomorrow." She knelt down and she said, "You mean good-bye." Then I knew I was in big trouble, because the one thing Lucy never said was, "Good-bye."

I started shaking. The limo pulled away and I turned in my seat to see Lucy standing in the driveway as we turned out of sight. I kept thinking, "Why did I go out? When I saw Paula in the backseat, why didn't I turn around and go back home? Why didn't I listen to Tom when he told me not to bring any of this up to Lucy?" Ambrose told me everything was going to be fine and kept calling me a dirt bag to try to jolly me back to life. When I finally calmed down I said to him, "Ambrose, you know what, you're absolutely right. Lucy will go to sleep and she'll be fine in the morning." And you know what, I was absolutely wrong.

After another mostly sleepless night, this time though in my own bed, I awoke to find an acerbic message Lucy left on our answering machine saying she was flying back to Los Angeles and I should not try to contact her ever again. "How could she do that?" I kept saying to Tom as I played and replayed the message over and over again as if it would change to something like, "Baby, everything is fine. I'll see you later for backgammon." My heart was breaking. Tom called Lucy at her apartment and made every excuse in the book for my inappropriate behavior but Lucy would have no part of any apology. When I got on the phone she hung up. That afternoon the moving company called to say they would be there the next day to take the boxes out.

In the spring of 1985 the Museum of Television and Radio, then called the Museum of Broadcasting, was planning a retrospective of Lucy's television and radio work. *I Love Lucy* was actually a spin-off of *My Favorite Husband*, a radio show costarring Richard Denning as her husband and featuring Gale Gordon and Bea Benaderet. When CBS wanted to transfer the show to television, Lucy stipulated she would do it only if Desi played her husband. After much reluctance from network brass and sponsors about casting a Cuban opposite an all-American redhead, they acquiesced and the rest is television history.

A gala dinner in Lucy's honor was planned to kick off a three-month series of *Lucy* shows at the museum on East Fifty-second Street. I was thrilled when Lucy asked me to work with her longtime California-based publicist Charlie Pomerantz in coordinating the gala. Lucy and I had already had a few meetings with Robert Batscha, the president of the museum, and Lettie Aronson (Woody Allen's sister), who was then doing public relations for the museum, and now produces her brother's films.

About ten days after Lucy returned to Beverly Hills, I received a telegram stating that my services for the retrospective and gala dinner were no longer needed. It also said that I was to immediately give Paula Stewart the set of keys I kept to Lucy and Gary's apartment. I thought *that* was really a low blow. The telegram was signed by Gary Morton, Executive Vice President, Lucille Ball Productions.

What made Lucy so angry with me? And why couldn't she forgive me? Surely people had arguments with her and lost their temper. Did she summarily cut them out of her life, too? And then I thought, Maybe that's exactly what Lucy did. When her daughter spoke her mind and it differed from what Lucy had in mind, there were always fireworks. Sometimes they wouldn't speak for weeks on end and I would be with Lucy and I would see how upset she was but she wouldn't give in. Desi Jr. just stayed away for long stretches at a time—not that mother and son were estranged. He just chose to speak to Lucy on the phone. Better for both of them, I guess. How long would it take for Lucy to come around and realize how much we meant to each other and put me back in her life?

Over the next few months Lucy spent a lot of time in New York—first preparing for the museum event for which she hired nobody to replace me, and then shooting *Stone Pillow* entirely on location in Manhattan. Lucy however spent no time with me. It was almost unbearable knowing she lived just a few blocks away and not seeing her. Occasionally I called the apartment and left a message on the machine when I knew she and Gary would be out. One time I called and when she answered, I got so flustered, I hung up. The calls were never returned, except once when Lucy called our apartment and deliberately left a message for Tom saying she was in town and hoped *he* was doing fine. There was no invitation to get together, however, and no mention of me. I had heard from time to time that Lucy could sometimes be intentionally cruel when she wanted to, especially when she knew you were vulnerable, but I dismissed it as myth. But now I was on the receiving end and it hurt a lot. I wrote notes and left them with her doormen. They were never answered.

Time away from Lucy did not heal anything. As the months went by without a word from her I grew convinced I was out of her life forever. When you have an argument with a friend nobody cares much. When you have an argument with Lucille Ball people notice. At first I downplayed our estrangement to friends saying Lucy was busy so we had less time together. After a while it became evident to everyone Lucy wasn't seeing me at all. Especially when I wasn't with her on the night the Museum of Broadcasting honored her.

Then one day, after a little more than a year of not seeing or hearing from Lucy, I received this handwritten letter:

> Dear Lee,
>
> My answer to your letters has been belated because of my arm. It is still difficult to write with it, and I did not want to dictate this to Wanda. However, I'm feeling very improved finally after three and a half months—diagnosed as dehydration, malnutrition, spastic colon, and blood pressure problems, along with enough little bits and pieces to make a mini-series.
>
> I'm still with my physiotherapist and trying to get my writing arm to find some strength—don't know how long that will be. Two broken tendons! Anyway, it's obvious it's hard for me to write. I liked getting your letters

and still miss the laughs we had—it was the most fun I had had in thirty years, but I'm not over the fright of your behavior. I have tried to forget it and/or minimize it but haven't been able to. You scared the hell outta me, and Paula and even Ambrose.

I can hardly read this myself, so gotta rest my arm. My love to both of you—glad everything is going so well for you.

My backgammon game is out the window. I cannot use my arm that much. That'll give you an idea. See you in N.Y.C. someday.

Love, Lucy

P.S. Hope you can read this.

I read the letter over and over again, looking for some sign between the lines that Lucy was ready to reconcile. "See you in N.Y.C. someday," I supposed was the best that I could hope for.

Lucy had met Mark and Betty Cohen at a private club in Beverly Hills when she was first learning to play backgammon. They moved to Florida and Lucy saw them when she and Gary visited Gary's mother, Rose, in North Miami Beach. Then the Cohen's moved to Manhattan and took an apartment just a few blocks from Lucy.

Betty and Lucy became very good friends and backgammon mates. Lucy always needed a close pal around, a confidante, and Betty fit the bill perfectly. She was a terrific gal—easygoing, agreeable, and she was there whenever Lucy needed her. Lucy might have liked her privacy, but unlike Garbo, she *never* wanted to be alone. Tom and I would also see lots of Betty Cohen even when Lucy wasn't in town. Betty felt awful about what happened between Lucy and me. I showed her the letter from Lucy and she was convinced that Lucy was "thawing." I wasn't so sure.

I wanted to call Lucy right away in California, but Betty suggested that I write to her instead, which I did the next day. Lucy never wrote back. In fact it would be some time before I saw her again.

Lucy & Me in NYC

DURING THE LAST DECADE OF HER life, Lucy was at her happiest in New York. I have do doubt about that. She felt free in the city, and although by no means anonymous, Lucy got around town like everyone else. She loved to walk. Sometimes we took a bus or hailed a taxi rather than have Amborse chauffeur her. Lucy loved *everything* about the city.

There are so many Manhattan memories: My favorite one is the time I took Lucy to the movies—the one and only time I took Lucy to the movies in New York. Here's why.

It was the Cinema One on Third Avenue and we walked the half-mile or so from Lucy's apartment. She was dying to see Shirley MacLaine in *Terms of Endearment*, so much so that she was willing to give up an afternoon of backgammon. It was a bitter cold Sunday in early March. On the walk down Third, Lucy told me she had not been in a movie theater in over twenty-five years, except when she attended a Hollywood pre-miere, which was rare. She recalled two occasions—the opening of *A Star Is Born*, with Garland, and the premiere of *Mame*. *Terms of Endearment* was an immensely popular film so when we got to the theatre, the ticket holder's line wound its way around the block. I told Lucy I would speak to the manager and I was sure we would be able to wait inside the lobby. "No way!!" Lucy said, and we stood on line in the cold with everyone else. I was freezing and pissed. Lucy was happy as a clam swathed in her Russian-lynx walking coat. Of course, Lucy drew throngs of folk around her all thrilled to freeze their asses off also and she loved every minute of amiably chatting with the people on line and passersby who recognized her. Lucy loved feeling "regular" and she made the most of it.

When we finally got inside, Lucy said she wanted to sit in the balcony and in the middle of the row. Another chance for her to feel "regular?" With Lucy, you never knew what to think. You just *did*. "And baby, get me a big bag of popcorn with lots of butter, and a diet Coke." She handed me one dollar.

"Keep your money, Auntie Mame," I said. And as I waved the dollar bill in front of her face I added "It has been a *long* time since you've been to the movies." Ten minutes later I came back to find Lucy signing autographs and holding court in the balcony of the Cinema One. She was almost squealing with delight. And with popcorn and sodas in hand we settled in our seats to watch the coming attractions.

"What the *hell* is this?" Lucy asked like she was talking at home.

I whispered, "Trailers."

"What?"

"Trailers, previews."

"Really?" She said.

"Yeah," I said, "and these are Talkies." She poked me hard in the ribs.

Soon the film began. The first scene of *Terms of Endearment* is a flashback of Shirley MacLaine going into her infant daughter's room and bending over the crib to see if her baby is breathing. Lucy asked out loud, "Is that Shirley MacLaine? It doesn't look like Shirley Maclaine?" We're in deep shit, I said to myself. Lucy spoke to me, and to herself out loud whenever she didn't hear something that was said on screen or understand something that was happening. Lucy or no Lucy, the audience started turning on her. We got a lot of "Shhhhhus" and "Would you please shut up?" And some teenagers behind us even started throwing popcorn. Lucy was oblivious and went right on talking with Shirley and Debra Winger.

The penultimate scene of the film is an emotionally gripping one; Debra is on her deathbed, and Shirley is screaming at the nurses to give some medication to her daughter. Lucy decides to take out her compact, one with chaser lights that flicker around the frame and she starts putting on lipstick. Everyone in the balcony is rapt and crying and Lucy wants to know if her lipstick is on right. I couldn't believe it. Anyway, Lucy loved the film and we saw it again at a screening for friends at home in Beverly Hills. And not surprisingly, Lucy went crazy when somebody talked during the film. And instead of popcorn and soda Lucy served iced water only. Lucy said that *Terms of Endearment* and *My Fair Lady* were the two best movies she had ever seen.

After *Terms*, I decided that movies would be best seen at home but Lucy still pulled that lighted compact stunt in every darkened Broadway and Off-Broadway theatre we went to. Lucy adored musicals and I wanted to go to lots of Broadway openings with Lucy. But she preferred to attend a preview or go the second or third night after opening. Her reasoning was twofold; first she was not fond of being photographed by the press, who would naturally be there on opening night. And second, Lucy was very sensitive about upstaging the star, which her presence was almost certain to do. Again, she wanted to be regular—just like everybody else sitting in a darkened theatre enjoying the show. The only difference was she applied makeup during the finale.

Lucy adored Tommy Tune. She loved absolutely everything about him—his Texas twang, the way he looked, all six-foot, six and a half inches of him, how he danced, how he directed. So when Lucy was in New York in the 1980s we made a point of seeing everything Tommy Tune did: *Nine, Cloud Nine,* and *My One and Only.* I had first met Tommy when he was directing and choreographing *The Best Little Whorehouse in Texas* on Broadway and I was the creative director for the advertising campaign. We were more acquaintances than we were friends, and we saw each other on occasion, usually at opening nights on Broadway.

One night after seeing one of his shows, Lucy, Tom, and I met Tommy for a late supper in a private dining room at the Helmsley Palace. Lucy was in great spirits that night and we all laughed and ate and drank a lot. Maybe we drank a little too much, considering the lateness of the hour. Tune, who I remembered as aloof and a bit standoffish, was very friendly and attentive to me that evening—which made me feel swell because, like Lucy, I was in awe of his talents.

Evidently, to Lucy, Tune and I were a little too friendly. We finished supper well after midnight and we were strolling through the lobby two by two; Tommy and Tom followed by Lucy and me. Lucy grabbed my arm, and applying some pressure to my biceps said "You've got one Tommy in your life, make sure it stays that way!"

Suddenly sobered up, I asked, "Lucy, what are you *talking* about?"

"You know baby, exactly what I'm talking about, and if you don't I'll *'splain* it to you tomorrow." When she said " *'splain,*" I knew no further explanation was needed.

When it came to spotting any kind of shenanigans, however

benign, Lucy had eyes in back of her head. Desi's years of blatant indiscretions had made her an expert in that department. And she was vociferous in telling people, sometimes perfect strangers, about his extramarital affairs. One evening at the Brasserie Restaurant, the same night she tripped on the stairway and almost fell into someone's French onion soup, two very elegantly dressed women were sitting in the next banquette. They, of course, noticed Lucy and struck up a conversation with her. It turned out that one of the women was from Santiago de Cuba, Desi's birthplace. The conversation turns to Desi, and the next thing you know, instead of extolling Desi's virtues as businessman and performing artist to these perfect strangers, Lucy, while sipping a bourbon and soda tells them about his excessive drinking and womanizing. It was one of those "You had to be there" stories, because Lucy wasn't angry or anything, there was no contempt in her tone—she was just matter-of-factly filling these women's unsuspecting ears with tales of Desi screwing every broad in Hollywood while they were married. These poor women didn't know what to say, so when Lucy finished her diatribe, they politely asked for her autograph, ordered dinner, and never spoke to us again.

Although Lucy did shy away from the glare of opening nights on Broadway, we did attend one in 1983. It was the Kander and Ebb musical, *The Rink* starring Liza Minnelli and Chita Rivera. Liza had personally phoned Lucy a few days before the opening and told her she *had* to be there. Lucy knew Liza since she was born, and had always been very fond of her and a big fan. Even as an adult, Liza looked upon Lucy as a "second mother," and in 1972, Lucy almost became Liza's mother-in-law when Liza was briefly engaged to Desi Arnaz Jr.

It was a star-studded black-tie opening, with Lucy looking sensational as usual with Tom and me on either arm. We took our fifth-row center seats. Lucy sat on my right and actress Patricia Neal on my left. I was always a big fan of Miss Neal's, ever since my grandmother took me to see her in *The Subject Was Roses* when I was a young boy. I introduced myself and spoke to her for some time before the show began. I then turned back to Lucy, who was applying lipstick for the umpteenth time and, with my tongue planted firmly in cheek, I told her how excited I was to be sitting next to a *real* movie star. Lucy gave me one of her classic, "What do I look like, chopped liver" looks as I tightly squeezed her hand. While at the same time trying unsuccessfully to wrestle away her chaser-light compact.

Opening night curtains always go up late. It's part of the mystique and excitement. But this one seemed later than usual. The buzz in the theatre was that the curtain was being held for Michael Jackson. Michael was at the peak of his popularity and had recently made front-page headlines when his hair went up in flames and he narrowly escaped being badly burned while filming a Pepsi-Cola commercial.

When I whispered to Lucy what I thought the delay was, she said, "Jeeeesus, maybe he's on fire again," loud enough for everyone in earshot to clearly hear. Even in fifth row center, Lucy could still break an audience up. As a first night concession to the stars, Lucy, thank God, refrained from putting on rouge, powder, or lipstick during the show, and waited instead for intermission. At the curtain calls Lucy stood and applauded long and loud for Liza, Chita, and the rest of the company.

The opening night party was at The Roxy roller rink in Chelsea, and surprisingly, Lucy said she wanted to go. Ordinarily, Lucy would want to go right home, get into a bathrobe, put her hair in rollers, play some backgammon, and call it a night. But that night she was going for Liza, and so off to the party we went. It was a typical Broadway opening night party; overcrowded, under catered, and almost impossible to get a drink. Upon our arrival we were immediately whisked to the VIP section where bodyguards hovered around Liza. It was very tight quarters and Lucy was getting nervous in the hot, noisy, and smoke-filled room. Over the din she yelled into my ear, "*shpilkas,*" which was Yiddish for "fidgety." Gary had told me that this was Lucy's password and when she said it you knew she needed to leave wherever she was in a hurry.

We got Lucy past Liza's entourage and saw Liza with her head resting in her hands like a kid in school taking a nap at recess. Lucy tapped her on the shoulder and Liza turned around, looked up, and shouted, "Mama, oh, mama, I'm so glad you're here!" They hugged each other for close to a minute, while Lucy kept whispering things in her ear. Then Liza buried her head in Lucy's neck and wept like a baby. On stage, earlier that evening Liza generated enough electricity to single-handedly light up Broadway! Now she looked exhausted, frail, and strung out. In the limousine on the way home Lucy stared out the window and cried.

My birthday is November 10, and somehow Lucy always managed to be in New York to celebrate it with me. If my birthday fell on a matinee day we would go to lunch and the theatre and make an afternoon of it. We always ate at the Oyster Bar on the lower level of Grand Central Station. It was one of Lucy's favorite restaurants, and she loved to sit in the back room, the Saloon. She always ordered the same thing. Oyster stew and an iced tea. After lunch she would sign autographs for all the waiters, many of whom looked like they had worked there since the first train pulled out of Grand Central.

Whenever Lucy and I dined out without Gary, I picked up the tab. Lucy would tell me to send the receipts to Wanda at the office so I would get reimbursed. I never bothered, although I knew Wanda would have sent the money in a minute. On one particular birthday, Lucy insisted on paying the bill, but she really didn't have a clue how to do it. So when the check came, Lucy took out her backgammon baggie filled with only dollar bills and counted them out one by one. After she counted to forty and dropped a few dollar bills on the floor and began recounting all over again, I suggested we use one of her credit cards, which were unsigned on the back and tied together with a rubber band at the bottom of her white handbag. After fiddling with the rubber band and sorting out her cards she decided to pay with her California driver's license. "Lucy, they only take American Express or Visa," I said, jokingly acknowledging the license she laid on the table. "Besides," I said, "The way *you* drive it will never get approved."

She didn't laugh and I think I embarrassed her because she threw the whole pack of cards at me and said, "Here, you pay the goddamn bill and leave a big tip. And don't forget to sign my name Lucille Ball Morton, and don't forget to get the money back from Wanda!" I didn't have the heart to tell her it was *her* credit card. She seemed so confused already.

Lucy and I had a post–Oyster Bar ritual. Right in front of the entrance to the restaurant, there are four stone arches, each diagonal from the other. If you go into one corner and barely whisper into the arched wall, the person at the opposite arch some thirty feet away can hear every word you say. It's some sort of architectural phenomenon. Lucy loved to stand against the wall and talk to me and nobody ever looked twice. Even Lucy was hard to recognize from behind, and besides in New York City it's not unusual for people to talk to themselves in

Grand Central Station.

After my birthday lunch Lucy and I were going to see *La Cage Aux Folles*. When we got to the Oyster Bar, she sent Ambrose and the limousine home for the day. Now we were on our own. "Wouldn't the subway be fun?" Lucy naively asked. "We could take the shuttle to Times Square like I used to when I first came to New York," she enthusiastically added.

"No, it would not be fun," I said, equally enthusiastically. I thought to myself, Could you just see Lucy and me on the subway—I would lose her, I know it and it would be just like the time Ethel lost Lucy on the subway when she had a loving cup stuck on her head. So we hailed a cab to the Palace Theatre.

Lucy was very excited about seeing the show. Gene Barry, one of the stars, was an old friend since the days when he was a regular on *Our Miss Brooks* starring Eve Arden and produced by Desilu. Years later, Barry was the star of the very successful television show *Bat Masterson*. Jerry Herman, the composer of *Mame*, wrote the score to *La Cage*, and the Palace Theater on Broadway and Forty-seventh Street itself held a very fond memory for Lucy: it was right outside the Palace that Lucy was first asked to go to Hollywood.

She was working in New York modeling dresses for designer Hattie Carnegie. On a sweltering day in July 1933, Lucy was walking by the theater when a casting agent she knew came out and told her that one of the girls hired by Samuel Goldwyn as a "Goldwyn Girl," his version of a "Ziegfeld Girl," had dropped out—and they needed somebody immediately to take her place. She said, "Yes," on the spot and the train for the coast left three days later with a not quite twenty-two-year-old Lucy on board. The next week she was a "Goldwyn Girl" in Hollywood, with a walk-on in *Roman Scandals*, her first film, starring the legendary Eddie Cantor.

La Cage was a big Tony Award—winning hit with standing room only. As usual, we had the best seats in the house. It didn't take long for the "bridge and tunnel" crowd, theater-goers coming in from Long Island and New Jersey, to recognize Lucy. Before the show began I waited in the inside lobby watching half the women seated in the orchestra follow Lucy into the ladies room. Lucy couldn't even take a pee in peace, I thought. You never saw so many people, all of whom had to go to the bathroom all at the same time.

At intermission we stayed in our seats. Lucy loved the show and was busily reading the *Playbill*. Everybody else's eyes were on her. I stood up at my seat and looked up at the mezzanine and balcony to see hundreds of people looking down at the redhead in the tenth row. The houselights began dimming for the start of the second act, when from the rafters came a lone male voice. "I love you, Lucy," he shouted down. That was it. From all over the theatre echoes of, "We love you, too, Lucy. Lucy, you're the greatest." And then more cheers and then thunderous applause and a standing ovation from everyone in the Palace Theater—the likes not heard, I'm sure, since Judy Garland played there.

All of a sudden the houselights went back up and the applause continued. I had never seen anything like it; so much adulation for someone sitting in the audience. Lucy was touched and truly bewildered by all the attention. She was still seated and did not know what to do. I told her she had to stand up and take a bow or the second act would never begin. When she did and waved to the crowd, the people went wild. In all the years I had been out in public with Lucy I had never seen anything like the idolatry she received that day at the Palace.

At the curtain call Lucy led a standing ovation for Gene Barry, George Hearn, and the rest of the cast. But it was nowhere as tumultuous as her own intermission applause. Lucy and I along with the company manager, press agent, and AP photographer rode a tiny elevator to Gene Barry's dressing room at the top of the theatre. Lucy knocked on the door and without a response entered. "So, 'Big Red,' are you happy now that you've upstaged me?" Gene said, embracing Lucy. "You got as much applause for sitting on your ass as I got for working mine off."

"Much more," Lucy answered with her usual impeccable comic timing. Everybody except Gene roared with laughter. The chorus boys still in drag rushed in and crowded around Lucy to get some shots with her. It was like Lucy's opening night, with Gene Barry resigned to take second billing. Lucy posed for pictures with anyone who could push his or her way into the dressing room. Lucy came alive in that dressing room and I thought about how I wished *Miracles* would have come true for her.

Charles Pierce was an incredibly talented female impersonator and a good friend of Lucy. She would catch his act on the West Coast whenever she could. During Lucy's last trip to New York in 1988, he was performing at a nightclub in Chelsea called the Ballroom, and Charlie called Lucy to ask her to come. Although at this time Lucy was slipping into a deep depression, if a performer, especially one she admired, requested her presence, Lucy would be there. Pierce was filming his act for home video release and Charlie wanted Lucy there for star support and for her fabulous and infectious laugh.

The Ballroom was an Art Deco nightclub with three levels of long tables that sat up to ten guests. Everything about the Ballroom fascinated Lucy. I think for her it harked back to the days when she and Desi frequented Manhattan nightspots like El Morocco, the Stork Club, the Copa, the Empire Room at the Waldorf, and the Plaza's Persian Room. Chita Rivera, Harvey Fierstein, and producer Leonard Soloway joined Tom, Lucy, and me at our table.

The houselights were dimming and Charles Pierce was about to make his entrance as Katharine Hepburn from the back of the house when Lucy whispered in my ear that they would have to stop filming the show because there was something wrong with the lighting. She started pointing at a particular fixture just as "Hepburn" came down the aisle with plastic cut flowers shouting, "The calla lilies are in bloom again, really they are," madly patting her hair bun as gobs of white powder flew everywhere. Charlie Pierce *was* Kate Hepburn and Lucy was hysterical. "But she's going to have to do it again, there's a fixture out," Lucy again whispered to me.

"Kate" continued regaling us with a story about how she just got attacked in Central Park by a group of gay men that demanded to do her hair and rearrange her flowers. We were in stitches when the director yelled, "Cut." There was a key light not functioning properly and it would have to be replaced. Lucy knew her stuff—why not, after making over seventy films and five hundred television shows.

Fifteen minutes later, lighting problem solved, "Hepburn" made her second entrance and it was as funny as the first because Lucy made sure she and everyone at our table laughed as loud and long as we did the first time. We had a wonderful evening, that evening, and Lucy laughed more than she had in a very, very long time.

A couple of days after we saw Charlie Pierce at the Ballroom, Lucy and I were playing backgammon at her apartment and the phone rang. Lucy hated answering the phone. Gary wasn't home so I picked it up. "Morton residence," I said, "Just a minute, please." I held my hand over the mouthpiece and whispered to Lucy that it was Charlie Pierce asking for her, doing his best Hepburn impersonation. Lucy picked up the phone, and did her best Tallulah. "Hello darling, how are you darling, isn't it a gorgeous day darling, what can I do for you today darling?" Sounding just like Tallulah when she was a guest star on the *Lucy-Desi Comedy Hour*.

Then suddenly Lucy's voice and manner changed completely and she started to have a normal conversation, albeit with clipped responses. "I do love being back in town." Pause. "Yes, that would be nice." Pause. "Just let me know, I'll be here another couple of weeks just playing backgammon. I'm not going anywhere." Pause. "You, too, dear, and God bless and thanks so much for the call."

Lucy hung up, lit a cigarette, and inhaled deeply as I started putting two and two together. "Lucy, who *was* that on the phone?" I asked, knowing almost for sure the answer.

"*Good God*, it was Kate," Lucy said. And then with a dead-on impersonation of Hepburn continued, "Lucy dear, someday soon I may rap, rap, rap on your dower, so we could talk and laugh, wouldn't that be such fun?" Then as Lucy, Lucy says, "Jeeesus, why the *hell* would she want to see me?"

"I don't know, maybe Florence Henderson isn't in town," I said. Lucy howled. "But I know one thing," I said, "If Miss Hepburn comes rap, rap, rapping at your dower and I'm not here, I'll rap, rap, rap you in the head!" Hepburn never did come rapping at Lucy's door.

George Schlatter, who brought *Laugh-In* to television in the 1960s, was in the 1980s producing an annual TV show called *Television Comedy Hall of Fame*. Each year, awards were bestowed on mainly the pioneers of the medium, and Lucy naturally was one of the first artists to be inducted. George asked Lucy to appear the following year and present the honor to Mary

Tyler Moore. Lucy declined, telling George she *had* to be in New York on business. It was partially true—she was coming east—but the real reason Lucy said no was that she hated to get "done up" for those shows. What with the wig and the netting and her facial skin pulled up practically over her head, and all the tons of makeup she insisted on wearing before she would face the camera. She would of course do it if she were receiving an honor, but to go on the air to give one was another story. Besides Lucy now had the apartment in New York and she was planning an extended trip to the city to see her boys (Tom and me) and play lots of backgammon. George replaced Lucy with Lily Tomlin, who was a *Laugh-In* alumna, and Bette Midler.

Lucy was in New York when they taped the show and still in town when the show aired a couple of weeks later. We were sitting in her living room playing backgammon, Tom, Lucy, and me, and watching the show at the same time. Actually Tom and I are watching, Lucy's back was to the television set.

Lily and Bette were introduced and the first thing they chatted about was that they were replacing Lucille Ball, who had a scheduling conflict. Lucy's only conflict at the moment was whether or not to give me the doubling cube. Lily said something like "I wish Lucy was here tonight, I would really love to meet her. I'm such a big fan."

Then Bette cockily said, "You mean you *never* met Lucy. I had tea one time with her at her Beverly Hills mansion."

Then I said, "Lucy did you hear what they're talking about? Listen!"

And Lucy said, "Keep your mind on the game, it's your move." So there was Bette Midler and Lily Tomlin going on and on about their comedic idol and there I was sitting opposite the idol herself, dressed in a flannel robe with her hair in rollers and a babushka on her head. Lucy finally turned her head and looked at the screen, muttered something under her breath, turned back to the board, and resumed play.

When Bette and Lily were through with their idolatry of Lucy she said she didn't want to watch anymore and we listened instead to Bobby Darin tapes. Lucy seemed preoccupied with something and a few minutes later she got up from the table and scribbled something on a notepad that she kept by the side of the phone. Later I looked: Lucy had written, "Call George and arrange lunch with B. & L."

When Lucy returned to California a few weeks later all three ladies did indeed lunch at Chasen's and Lucy called me right after she got home to tell me everything that happened. She knew I would be jealous as hell so she really laid it on. But she made it up to me; the next time I came out to the coast, Lucy took me out to dinner, where we dined with Bob Newhart, Don Rickles, and Sammy Davis Jr. It was the first and last time I ate out with celebrities in Beverly Hills.

Lucy loved to window-shop on Madison Avenue and take long strolls through Central Park, especially in the dead of winter. She'd put on her mink or sable, tie a cashmere scarf around her head, don a big pair of sunglasses which practically covered her entire face, and off we'd go onto the streets of Manhattan. Everybody recognized her no matter what she wore. How could they not? The *Guinness Book of World Records* says, "The face of Lucille Ball has been seen by more people, more often, than the face of any human being who ever lived." People stared but rarely approached her. They would just stop dead in their tracks and watch her as she walked by. Lucy would just hold onto my arm very tight and made eye contact with no one. She wasn't being aloof. She was just not used to being outside among people and a bit overwhelmed by it all.

Lucy loved hot dogs, the big fat "Specials" they served with baked beans at P. J. Bernstein's, a delicatessen on Third Avenue right around the corner from her apartment. And pastrami sandwiches on rye with mustard and a cream soda. So after the Beverly Hills beans and franks fiasco I suggested we eat lunch out whenever we could. Lucy's favorite dinner was meatballs and spaghetti at Carino restaurant on Second Avenue and Eighty-eighth Street right across the street from Elaine's, where Lucy and Gary used to hang out before I began hanging out with her.

Every Sunday evening right after watching 60 *Minutes*, like clockwork, we would go for meatballs and spaghetti. Carino was an unpretentious little hole-in-the-wall with red-and-white checked tablecloths and corny paintings of Sicilian scenes on the walls. Like Tony's, the Italian joint Lucy and Ethel went to when Ethel disguised herself as one part American Indian, one part Japanese geisha, and one part Eskimo. "Mama" Carino, in her seventies at the time (and still cooking today at ninety), would personally supervise the kitchen. Every Sunday after giving "Mama" a big hug and kiss, Lucy would sit at the front table by the window waving to any unsuspecting passerby who caught her eye while she was chowing down on meatballs and spaghetti.

I think Lucy loved New York best because everyday she got to do all the things nobody let her do in Beverly Hills or Palm Springs. Lucy insisted on doing her own housework. So one morning when her bathtub overflowed while she was talking to me on the phone, she tried to use the Dustbuster to vacuum up the water. Thank God the wall switch that controlled the electricity was shut off.

Lucy wanted to do her own grocery shopping at The Food

Emporium, a supermarket a couple of blocks away from her apartment. There was no way I could let her go alone. So once a week Lucy would push her shopping wagon down the narrow aisles and she could not for the life of her understand why the aisle where she was shopping was so crowded when the rest of the store was so empty. Finally, we created a diversion—I left Lucy alone for a few minutes with her shopping cart and fans while I got everything she needed and checked them out in no time flat, since hardly anybody was at the checkout counter when Lucy was in the store. When I was through I would collect Lucy, who would then leave her shopping cart with all her bogus groceries right in the middle of the aisle. The customers would have a field day grabbing the box of Cream of Wheat that Lucille Ball had touched.

Lucy got such a big kick out of riding in elevators, again something she rarely did in California except for an occasional visit to her production office on Sunset Boulevard. She was like a little kid who if I had let her would have pressed all the buttons just to watch the elevator door open and close on every floor. She especially liked riding in the elevator of her apartment building. And when we were in the elevator together and somebody else would come in, Lucy would position herself directly behind me, and as we were quietly watching the numbers change from floor to floor Lucy would goose me. Not all the time—just often enough to keep me guessing when she would do it again. So in anticipation of Lucy's goose, I'd start giggling and Lucy would look at me like I was nuts. She would even pretend she didn't know who I was and say things like, "Sir, is there something wrong, can I help you?" And then her hand would be all over my backside.

There was a company called Blackglama that manufactured fur coats and was especially known for its Blackglama Mink print advertising campaign. The magazine ads featured very famous celebrities—the kind that did not need their name under their photograph in order to know who they were—wearing Blackglama Mink. Above their image was the line, "What Becomes a Legend Most." Audrey Hepburn, Angela Lansbury, Shirley MacLaine, Claudette Colbert, Diana Ross, Carol Channing, Bette Davis, even Tommy Tune, posed for full-length photos and their take-home salary was taking home a Blackglama Mink coat.

I had wanted Lucy to be a part of this campaign for as long as I could remember—way before we became such good friends. Blackglama wanted her, too, but Lucy had always turned them down. The campaign was produced in New York and now that Lucy lived there, at least part time, I did a full-court press to get her to agree to do an ad. Peter Rogers, the genius behind the campaign, was a friend of a friend and I found out that he was still very interested in adding Lucy to his roster of legends. "Why the *hell* would they want me for?"

"Oh, I don't know," I said, "Maybe because Florence Henderson turned them down?"

Lucy laughed, "What's with you and Florence Henderson?" Then she told me to talk to Peter Rogers.

Peter was thrilled when I assured him that Lucy would say "Yes." I was going out on a limb. He decided that the best way to show off legendary Lucy in the ad was to capture her clown-like persona. I told him I could not agree more. If she would go for the idea we wanted to blacken out a couple of Lucy's front teeth and really tease and tousle her hair, so she'd look the way she did when she portrayed "The Queen of the Gypsies," Lucy's favorite I *Love Lucy* episode. I talked to Lucy about our notion and without hesitation she thought it was terrific—which surprised the hell out of me because Lucy never readily agreed to *anything*.

I realized that the look we were creating for Lucy must have appealed to her since the comedic disguise would make her worry less about her appearance in front of the camera. Also, she wouldn't have to wear one of those wigs with her skin painfully pulled under the netting for hours on end. Bill King, a leading fashion photographer, was going to shoot Lucy and the equally eminent Way Bandy was creating Lucy's makeup and hair for the black-and-white photo. Lucy never heard of either one of them, and at first insisted on her own hair and makeup people. But after some reassuring from Peter, Lucy put herself in his hands. She called Thelma Orloff on the West Coast, and given Lucy's predilection for malapropisms told Thelma that Hal King was photographing her (Hal King was her makeup man on *I Love Lucy*) and that a fellow named Gay Bandit was doing her hair and makeup.

The photo session was set and I was going to accompany Lucy to Bill King's lower Fifth Avenue studio. Then Gary entered the picture. Gary said he thought about the whole thing and told Lucy that she should go completely against type for this ad—she should opt for a sophisticated glamorous look instead of the madcap one that was agreed upon. I vehemently disagreed but Gary insisted and Lucy ultimately took his advice. Peter, Bill, and Way were very disappointed and tried to change Gary's and Lucy's minds. I decided not to go with Lucy to the shoot and Gary went instead, which meant missing a day of golf.

I heard that the shoot was a disaster. Lucy was a nervous wreck and drove everybody crazy. Gary held Lucy's hand and reassured her. She blamed him for getting her involved in the first place. Way's makeup was much too heavy and in the end Lucy looked mummified. The coat never fit right on her body no matter how they draped or pinned it. In fact it wasn't even a coat at all—just some skins loosely sewn together. Bill King captured abject terror on Lucy's face rather than sophistication. The photos turned out terrible—they were neither glamorous nor sophisticated but unintentionally humorous. Lucy hated them. She approved one shot for publication and when Lucy asked me my opinion of the photograph, which she already knew, I said it looked fine. The shot appeared in magazines for about a year and then it was pulled. It was a missed opportunity at what I think could have been the finest Blackglama print ad ever produced.

Gary and I disagreed on virtually everything when it came to what was right professionally for Lucy in the last decade of her life. From the start I never had very much respect for Gary, nor did I like him very much, I don't know why. I guess I should have been grateful that he married Lucy or I never would have met her at all. Anyway, I don't think he liked me all that much either. Other than both loving Lucy, we had nothing in common and he seemed to have no interest in being with me when Lucy wasn't around. When Lucy was around I made life a lot easier for her and that made life easier for him. After Lucy died I saw Gary once more and then never again.

I first clashed with Gary in 1982 when Alexander H. Cohen, the legendary producer and showman, was putting together *Night of 100 Stars*, a benefit for the Actors' Fund of America. Alex's intention was to get one hundred celebrities on board for a show at Radio City Music Hall—a night of song, dance, and comedy. He got more than he bargained for. Almost two hundred luminaries including James Cagney, Bette Davis, Elizabeth Taylor, Gene Kelley, Helen Hayes, Liza Minnelli, the New York Yankees, and Princess Grace entertained a sold-out crowd of over six thousand people.

I was working on the advertising campaign for the event and I told Alex that I was not only sure Lucy would do *Night* of 100 *Stars* but I was positive she'd do one of the public-service radio spots we were producing to promote the gala. I was wrong on both counts.

Strange as this sounds, Gary had convinced Lucy that her absence from doing *Night of 100 Stars* would be more conspicuous than her presence. He said he didn't want Lucy to be among all those lesser known celebrities. When I told him who was on board he just shook his head. Stranger yet, Lucy listened to him and she turned down a chance to be part of an unforgettable event, which garnered worldwide publicity. When Lucy read the reviews of the show in the trade papers the next day, she didn't talk to Gary for a week.

Our next disagreement came in 1984 when Ellen Krass, an independent producer of film and theater, approached me and said she wanted to do a documentary on Lucy—her life and her work—with an on-screen narration by Lucy herself. I took a calculated risk and wrote a treatment for the show without first going to Lucy, which Ellen then took to both PBS and HBO. We got a green light from HBO, then a fledgling network, and some seed money to start research and preproduction. I then went to Lucy and explained what we were thinking and gave her the treatment to read. She was very excited about the proposed project but she definitely did not want to appear on camera. I was disappointed but asked her if she would consider an off-camera narration, which would still keep the essence of the film—Lucy talking about her life and her work strictly from her point of view. She readily agreed to that.

I told Lucy up front that there was very little money for anybody associated with *Lucy, Seriously Speaking*, the tentative title of the ninety-minute documentary. Money did not matter, Lucy said, as long as she had final say over which film clips were used and especially what was said about Desi Arnaz.

"Remember baby," she said "There would be no *Lucy* without Desi." She was thrilled that I was writing the documentary but said she would decide how much work I did every day compared to how much backgammon we played. At least she had her priorities straight.

Gary wanted no part of any show unless the producers agreed to pay an exorbitant fee to Lucille Ball Productions. He told Ellen that Lucy was the most famous person in the world and he wasn't about to "sell her out" for under a million dollars. This was ludicrous and after Gary and Lucy spoke privately Lucy changed her mind and the project was killed. Lucy somehow seemed relieved. I wondered if she ever wanted to do the show in the first place or she was just doing it for me. In any case, I was devastated and I told Lucy so. She said we would do something together someday. But we never did.

After Lucy died, Lucie Arnaz and Larry Luckinbill produced a terrific Emmy Award–winning documentary called *Lucy and Desi: A Home Movie*, which was later released for home video and which included no interviews with Gary. CBS did a dreadful movie of the week about Lucy and Desi starring Frances Fisher as Lucy, over which Gary had no approval. And PBS as part of their American Masters series produced a documentary called "Finding Lucy," a year after Gary Morton's death, about the life and work of Lucille Ball.

What was Lucy thinking when she relied on and trusted Gary's judgment? It's always mystified me. Perhaps Lucy needed to be taken care of so badly that she let Gary make decisions that were certainly not in her best interests. Perhaps she had been so used to Desi making the *right* decisions, she assumed Gary would do likewise. Or perhaps, and most likely, Lucy knew Gary's limitations and giving him some sense of authority was her way of making him feel worthy.

Lucy & Christmas

IN 1981 I SPENT THE FIRST OF MANY
holiday seasons with Lucy—Christmas in Beverly Hills, New
Year's in Palm Springs. When I was first invited out for the
holidays I had visions of Lucy's house on Roxbury Drive
adorned with a huge wreath on the front door. A great big
Christmas tree in the living room with lots of fancy gift-
wrapped presents under it, candles glowing in all the windows, maybe even a Santa and his reindeer on the front lawn.
Lucy loved the change of seasons so much that I imagined her
home transformed, so that regardless of the weather it would
look and feel more like Christmas in Jamestown, New York,
than in Southern California.

I arrived in Los Angeles on Christmas Eve day and the temperature was eighty-eight degrees in the shade. The front
lawns of gracious mansions that dotted Sunset Boulevard had
make-believe snow while Japanese gardeners pruning jasmine
and honeysuckle mopped real sweat from their brow. And
Lucy's house off Sunset stood out from all the rest—it had
absolutely no Christmas decorations of any kind.

I rang the side doorbell and when nobody answered I let
myself in. The house was very quiet. When I walked into the
dining room I startled Choo, the Chinese housekeeper, who

was wrapping a single gift on the dining room table. It was a tie for her husband Kum, Lucy's and Gary's chef. I distinctly remember that narrow box because it was the only one on that great big table. Where were the presents under the tree? Hell, where was the tree? The place was so still that the only sound you heard came from a small portable radio down the hall in the servants' quarters. It was Rosemary Clooney singing "White Christmas." Or it might have been Rosemary Clooney singing "White Christmas" from her home across the street on Roxbury. Choo wished me a Merry Christmas in English and in Chinese, which made me laugh. She said that Mr. Morton was playing golf and Missy Morton was upstairs resting. I told her not to wake her and I took my bags into the guesthouse.

I unpacked quickly and I decided to wash the long flight off with a quick dip in the pool. When my head surfaced above water, I squinted up into the blazing sun and saw a figure hovering over me dressed all in black with a Santa mask and beard and rolled up orange hair. "Santa Lucia," I cried out.

"Ho, Ho, Ho, I think we need a little Christmas now," Santa Lucia cried back, and with that she burst into an a cappella rendition of "We Need a Little Christmas" from *Mame*. "Haul out the holly, put up the tree before my spirits fall again," in a voice sounding much more like Tallulah than Santa. "Guess who?" Wailed Lucy from behind the mask.

"There's only one person I know who sings *that* off key," I fired back. Lucy kicked off her black ballet slippers and kicked water in my face. Hooray, I thought, I had finally found my Christmas spirit and her name was Lucy.

Of all the years spent with Lucy at Christmastime, the one I cherish most of all was the day before Christmas in 1988. I don't know, maybe it was because it *was* the last Christmas we shared, although at the time I certainly didn't expect it to be. Anyway, after my traditional arrival at 1000 N. Roxbury Drive, Lucy announced, "We're not playing backgammon today, we're going shopping."

"The heat must be getting to me," I said, "I thought I heard you say we weren't playing backgammon, we were going shopping."

"Don't be funny," Lucy shot back, "Or I won't take you to Rodeo Drive."

Lucy wanted to get some last-minute gifts—actually Lucy, as usual, had not done any personal Christmas shopping at all. She rarely did. So off we went in her Mercedes sedan for some last-minute gifts. It was the first and only time I ever drove with Lucy, and I thank God I lived to tell the story. The trip to bountiful Rodeo started when Lucy backed out of the driveway while putting on her lipstick. Instead of looking for traffic, she was looking at her lips in the rearview mirror and we nearly careened into a busload of tourists. "Lucy!" I screamed, "You almost slammed into that bus."

"So what, they all want to meet me anyway," Lucy chuckled.

We went down Roxbury to Sunset where we had to cross four lanes of traffic in order to get across the boulevard with no traffic light, just a stop sign for us. Rather than stop, Lucy at best yielded the right of way. She explained to me that when there was not much traffic, a stop sign was just like a yield sign. "Really?" I replied. Lucy's idea of not much traffic was cars barreling toward us from both directions. One guy in a Bentley slammed on his brakes, gave Lucy the finger, and then recognizing her turned it into a wave. I had never seen anything like that.

Continuing on Roxbury, south of Sunset, Lucy made a few sudden turns. First left, then right, then left again, totally ignoring the four-way stop signs as we wove our way through the residential streets of Beverly Hills. Lucy became my personal tour guide and pointed out the stars' homes usually with one hand on the wheel, and the other one flailing about. If she was showing me an unusually big or famous home she would take both hands off the steering wheel altogether. If her Mercedes veered into oncoming traffic, the cars would just have to work around her. And they did.

We finally reached Rodeo Drive, which looked a lot like Madison Avenue, only cleaner and with palm trees. It had practically all the same stores, but unlike its Manhattan equivalent the shoppers were suntanned, and you were bound to see a celebrity every ten minutes or so. Of course the biggest celebrity of all was sighted and seated right beside me behind the wheel. All of a sudden, Lucy spotted a space on the street, a rather tight one, and when she told me that she hadn't parallel parked in thirty-five years, I suggested she get out of the car and let me park for her.

Nothing doing. Lucy was going to parallel park. So I got out and assisted. Here we go again, I said to myself, another *I Love Lucy* episode. She was *Lucy* behind the wheel and I was Ricky teaching her to drive. The only difference was that I couldn't yell at her in Spanish.

At first a crowd gathered to see who the crazy redhead was frantically turning the steering wheel back and forth while the car lurched backward and forward as I screamed directions, which she totally ignored. When they realized who the crazy redhead was, the crowd got so thick you couldn't walk or drive down Rodeo. Vehicular traffic was backed up for blocks. Finally, Lucy parked, albeit two feet from the curb, but at least things got moving again. Everybody cheered, Lucy graciously bowed, and order was restored to Beverly Hills.

Lucy took out her shopping list. In her handwriting, was written: buy Gary a "Perry Como" sweater. A "Perry Como" sweater, for those of you under fifty, was a long-sleeved solid colored cardigan so named because Perry Como always wore one on his television shows. I think when Perry stopped making his music, they stopped making his sweaters, because I haven't seen them in stores for years.

Lucy needed gifts for her grandchildren. Her oldest, Simon Thomas, who was named for Neil Simon (Lucie and Larry were in Neil Simon plays when they met; Lucie in *They're Playing Our Song*, Larry in *Chapter Two*) and for Lucie's good friend Tommy Tune, whom she first met when they did *Seesaw* together. Kate, Lucy's youngest grandchild, who was named after Katharine Hepburn, and whose first name was spelled the same way Hepburn spelled hers with an *a* in the middle instead of an *e*. And Joseph Henry, Lucy's middle grandchild whose proper name was after no one in particular but whose middle name was Henry, for Henry Fonda, one of Lucie's favorite actors. When Lucie told her mother her grandson's full name she knew Mom would be very pleased because Lucy loved Henry Fonda very much. "Oh, Lucie," she interrupted, "I'm so grateful . . . so proud you kept the family name." At first Lucie didn't know what her mother was talking about and then she realized that Lucy thought she named him Henry after *her* father Henry Durrell Ball, who died when she was just four years old. Lucie never told her mother otherwise.

Lucy got the sweater for Gary, denim outfits for her grandkids, a silk scarf for her daughter, a pair of pajamas for her son-in-law Larry—all in about fifteen minutes. There really wasn't much joy in the buying. It was as if Christmas shopping was an obligation not a pleasure. Lucy bought the first item the salesperson showed her. She presented her credit card, not her driver's license, and I signed the sales slip Lucille Ball Morton and we left. As we walked back to the car, we passed a man's clothing shop with an absolutely gorgeous chocolate brown, cashmere sport coat in the window. "How do you like it?" Lucy asked.

"Are you kidding? I love it."

"Let's go in," she said, "Maybe you'll see something you like even better." We went in and spent almost an hour looking at and trying on different jackets until we bought the one I'd seen in the window. Lucy took a lot of pleasure in picking out that gift and she made me feel very special.

I couldn't bear the ride back home with Lucy at the wheel so I begged her to let me drive. "All right, but drive very carefully."

"Yes, Lucy," I replied dutifully. Even Lucy knew how ridiculous that advice sounded coming from her. We were on our way home when Lucy announced she wanted an ice-cream soda, and practically yanked the steering wheel from my hand so I could make a quick right turn.

"I know, let's go the Fountain Room at the Beverly Hills Hotel," she said. And the next thing you know we're swiveling on our stools sipping black and white ice-cream sodas through a straw on Christmas Eve. It felt like a scene from *Mame*.

That evening Gary, Lucy, and I drove to Lucie and Larry's home in Brentwood. Someone on the car radio was singing, "Have yourself a merry little Christmas." "I hate all female singers!" Lucy said turning down the volume.

Here we go again, I thought. "Lucy, what do you mean, you hate *all* female singers. You *love* Barbra Streisand. And what about Garland and Lena Horne?"

Lucy turned to me in the backseat and exasperatingly said, "Those are actresses who sing, Jeeesus, don't you know anything?" And that ended *that* conversation. And then she changed her tone completely. "Why don't we sing something from *Mame?*" So Lucy croaked out the verse to "If He Walked into My Life," and then I sang "Gooch's Song," every word, while Lucy howled and Gary drove.

The Luckinbill's Brentwood home, which they had moved into a year earlier, was perched high in the hills and had a commanding view of the City of Angels. Lucie is a terrific cook and marvelous hostess and she fixed a Christmas Eve buffet turkey dinner with all the fixings. Larry's two kids, Nick and Ben, from his first marriage to actress Robin Strasser joined us for dinner. The meal was absolutely delicious, and all through the night Lucy extolled her daughter's virtues. She'd turn to me and say, "I don't know how she has time to do *everything*—have a career, take care of a family, run a house. I *never* did what she does." Lucy was right. She was too busy running a studio instead.

We exchanged gifts right after dessert and then Lucy got *shpilkas* so we beat a hasty retreat. If there was little joy in the buying of the presents, there was even less joy in the giving. Lucy's uneasiness about sharing her love with her immediate family was palpable. I could never understand it because, believe me, Lucy could be a loving and deeply caring woman, who was capable of incredible gestures of kindness and generosity, often times to people she hardy knew. But when it came to risking intimacy, especially with her children and grandchildren, Lucy emotionally shut down.

We got home and played backgammon until the stroke of midnight. Gary went to bed. As Christmas Eve turned into Christmas Day Lucy stopped playing, leaned back in her chair, and ruefully reflected on Christmases past. She told me that what she missed most at the holidays was not being with her own mother, DeDe, who died in 1977. She talked about what Christmas was like with Desi when the kids were small—the friends and family who came for dinner, the presents under the tree, and most of all the laughter that rang through the house. She looked around the room then said, "Not much Christmas spirit left now, baby, is there? But at least I have you. Do you know how important you are in my life?" I reached across the backgammon table and gave Lucy a big hug.

"Let's call it a night," she said. I began to shut the lights in the lanai but Lucy said she wanted to just sit there alone for a while. I kissed her forehead and told her how much I loved her. I walked through the garden toward the guesthouse. I looked back to see a single light left burning in the lanai. There, Lucy sat alone, on early Christmas morning, just staring into space.

Seven years earlier, on my first Christmas Day with Lucy I awoke about ten o'clock and went into the house for some breakfast. Not a creature was stirring, except me stirring my coffee. It was almost too quiet. Kum and Choo were off with their family. Gary had gone out to drive some golf balls and left me a note telling me that Lucy turned off her phone and to please take any calls. Lucy and Gary did not have an answering machine. Remember, Lucy and Gary didn't even have Touch-Tone phones.

I sat in the kitchen eating a bialy with cream cheese feeling very homesick, wanting nothing more than to be in New York with all my friends, so I could go to the movies and eat shrimp and lobster sauce for dinner like every good Jew did on Christmas Day. Tom, as always, was in Memphis celebrating Christmas with his family and he was going to join Gary, Helen, Lucy, and me in Palm Springs later in the week. I had heard wonderful things about the California desert and I was eager to spend my first New Year's Eve there with Lucy.

The phone rang a lot that morning, and it was an absolute hoot taking calls from Dinah Shore, Betty White, Merv Griffin, June Havoc, and Gale Gordon—all calling to wish Lucy a Merry Christmas and to thank her for the beautiful clock they received. Wasn't it odd, I thought after the seventh call, everybody got a clock.

I found Wanda's home phone number in Gary's celebrity Rolodex and called to wish her a Merry Christmas and to find out the mystery of all the Christmas clocks. Wanda just chuckled and said Lucy liked to give clocks and watches to everybody. Lucy would write a note with each clock that said things like, "I'll always have time for you." Or, "There's never a time I don't think of you." And the note was signed "Love Lucy." I wondered if Carol Burnett's clock note said, "I'm so glad we had this time together."

Lucy came downstairs around noon—jogging suit on, hair in rollers, pocketbook in hand. There was a comfort in knowing that even on holidays Lucy didn't dress up. But her spirits were up as she announced that there would be a Christmas/Chanukah backgammon tournament and barbecue in my honor in the pool house at five o'clock. "Burgers and latkas for everyone in the house," Lucy cheered. The holiday invitees included Pat and Charlie Stone, Thelma Orloff, Jeanine Foreman, Mark and Betty Cohen, Helen, Gary, Lucy, and me.

Christmas Day in Beverly Hills was sunny and hot, not like the ones I used to know. After Lucy and I ate our grilled cheese sandwiches, which were paper thin and cut up in thirds, which Lucy insisted on making, and took forty-five minutes to prepare and five minutes to eat, we played backgammon in the pool house. Oh, how I loved looking at all those *Mame* pictures, hanging on the wall. I pointed to one I particularly liked—a shot of Lucy and some guys dancing during rehearsal. "God, it was a hundred and fifteen degrees the day we did that number," Lucy said, always being a bit prone to exaggeration. "Get a load of me with my shirt hanging out of my riding pants, and the kid in back with no shirt on at all."

The next thing I knew she took the photograph off the wall, inscribed the back "For Lee, Merry Christmas, 1981, Love Lucy," and gave it to me. I told Lucy it was the best Christmas gift I had ever gotten and I meant it. It was also the first of more than a dozen *Mame* photos that over the next eight years Lucy took of the wall, inscribed, and gave to me as gifts. But the best present of all arrived at my home on my thirty-eighth birthday, the last one Lucy celebrated with me. It was a full-length portrait in oil of Lucy as *Mame* blowing a bugle, which was originally done for the movie but replaced during production. Gary's pal, Lew Rudin, had bought it from Lucy as a gift to his wife and when they divorced the painting somehow came back to California where it sat in storage for nearly ten years.

Later that afternoon Lucy's backgammon mentor, Gaby Horowitz, stopped by the house. Lucy invited him over so I could play a few games of backgammon with him. Gaby was a brilliant player. I was so nervous in his presence I had all I could do just to remember what direction my men were moving. We played about a dozen games. Lucy said she wanted to watch. She wanted me to have a good time. I lost eleven out of twelve games. He threw the last one.

In 1989, Gaby Horowitz was accidentally shot by his good friend, Scientology minister Bruce Reamar, while the two were admiring a Colt. 45. Gaby was left brain-damaged and forced to use a wheelchair. When I met him he was married to Marcia Clark, who later gained prominence as the lead prosecuting attorney in the O. J. Simpson murder trial. Watching the trial on television in 1995, I often thought of Lucy and how hooked she would have been on the proceedings. This was just the kind of stuff that intrigued her. She even liked to watch Divorce Court.

Lucy was saying good-bye to Gaby when Thelma Orloff pulled into the driveway early. Whenever Lucy had a tournament, Thelma was always the first to come and the last to leave. This made Lucy nuts. "Jeeeesus, is fatso here already?" And of course Thelma's black Cadillac in the driveway was blocking Gaby's Porsche. So anticipating a directive, I asked Thelma if she wanted me to move her car. "Thanks baby and would you bring me a tall glass of iced tea out to the pool house with lemon and one Sweet'n Low on your way back you know I love you?" She said in one breath.

Everybody else came on time and they all thanked Lucy for their clocks. Thelma brought beluga caviar, which Lucy adored. Pat and Charlie brought a bottle of champagne, which Lucy adored. Jeanine brought a poinsettia plant, which Lucy despised. Unfortunately, the plant stayed out and the champagne and caviar went into the refrigerator unopened and not to be consumed, that day anyway. There was five minutes of small talk and then Lucy told everybody to shut up and the tournament began.

Earlier in the day I had suggested to Lucy that we set up a bar in the pool house. "What the hell for?" Lucy asked and answered. "We'll have iced water. It's good at Christmas." I asked Lucy if I could be in charge of cooking the franks and hamburgers on the outdoor barbecue grill and after much consternation she agreed. "Now you know you have to wait for the coals to get hot before you start grilling. And don't put the buns on until the meat is cooked. And don't stand too close to the fire, you'll get burned."

"Maybe you want to cook the hot dogs?" I coyly suggested. Lucy threw me one of her, "Don't be a smart-ass looks," she threw so well.

We had a terrific evening. Thelma won fifty dollars and was very happy. Dinner was delicious, and the hamburgers and hot dogs went down well with water. Everybody was gone by ten o'clock and Gary went upstairs to bed.

Lucy asked if I wanted a nightcap. No, not a snifter of brandy, just another game of backgammon. We were back into the lanai and I excused myself for a minute or two and went into the guesthouse. "Merry Christmas, Auntie Mame," I said, as I came back in and gave Lucy her Christmas present.

"Why, thank you Patrick," Lucy quipped as she madly un-wrapped her present. I had found an old photo of Lucy from her Hattie Carnegie modeling days in New York. She couldn't have been more than twenty-two. It was a black-and-white close-up of Lucy wearing a cashmere coat with the collar up around her face. I had the photo sepia-toned, a process that gives the print an antique-like quality and put it in a sterling silver frame from Cartier. The inscription read, Merry Christmas Lucy, With Love, Lee. She cried and put it on the table next to where we played backgammon, where it stayed until the day she died.

The day after Christmas I told Lucy I wanted her to meet a very special friend of mine who lived nearby in West Holly-wood. His name was Fritz Friedman and we became good pals when he lived in New York. Reluctant to put Lucy on the spot, and knowing how she guarded her privacy at home, I nevertheless asked her if it was all right if Fritz came by the house that afternoon. "Fritz Friedman?" Lucy asked. "How well do you know him?"

"Very well," I replied.

"Very well then," she replied back, "Tell him to come over. And bring a bathing suit. Does he know how to play backgammon, because we're playing backgammon all day?"

Fritz Friedman had an interesting heritage. His paternal grandfather was a Viennese Jew who migrated to New York City and ended up in Manila where he fought in the Spanish-American War. He married a Filipina. Their son, Fritz's dad, also married a Filipina and Fritz was the issue of that relationship. So Fritz Friedman was one quarter Jewish, looked Filipino, and was reared a Catholic. And he stood five feet five and one half inches tall.

I called Fritz and told him to come by around twelve-thirty. That way he could have Lucy's Blue Plate special—a grilled American cheese sandwich, one slice thick, on white toast with iced tea. Kum and Choo were home but off from work until that evening, so I told Fritz to come in the side door, which was left unlocked, and walk through the lanai into the garden where he would see Lucy and me in the pool house. Unbeknownst to me Gary had come home early from golf and was talking on the phone in the lanai when Fritz walked in. Gary repeatedly dismissed him with a wave of his hand and pointed him towards the servant's quarters, thinking he was a guest of Kum and Choo's, and Fritz repeatedly waved back thinking this was Gary's way of welcoming him.

Lucy greeted Fritz with an extended arm and a firm handshake as Fritz, uncharacteristically timid, said, "Hello, Miss Ball."

"My friends call me Lucy," said Lucy, hoping to put a visibly frightened Fritz right at ease. But she only succeeded in scaring him more. Lucy wasted no time. "So what do you do, Fritz?" Fritz quietly told her he worked in publicity for Columbia Pictures. "Speak up, how the hell is anybody going to know what Columbia's up to if they can't hear you?" Lucy said.

"I was wondering why nobody was going to our movies," Fritz spoke up. Lucy laughed out loud. Fritz's face lit up. He had passed the Lucy intimidation test. Lucy liked Fritz right away and she kept on telling him he didn't look anything like his name. Finally, Fritz told Lucy *she* didn't look anything like Lucille Ball.

We all ate our grilled cheese and then Fritz watched Lucy and me play backgammon. Then Lucy asked him to stay for dinner. Actually in true Lucy style, she ordered him rather than invited him. And later, somewhere between the Waldorf salad and the veal with vermicelli, Fritz matter-of-factly proclaimed, "You know, Lucy, you *are* a gay icon."

"Lucy, this veal tonight is delicious," I interrupted, trying to deflect the conversation, not because I cared in the least that Fritz was openly talking about being gay, but because I had a feeling where Fritz was headed.

"Fritzie, what the hell are you talking about?" Lucy barked.

Fritz continued. "Gay men adore you. You must know that. And you know, there's this gay bar on Santa Monica in West Hollywood where all weekend long they show I *Love Lucy* episodes day and night."

Gary perked up. "Luce, can they do that without your permission?" We all shot Gary a look.

"Anyway," Fritz added, "Wouldn't it be fun if Lee and I took you there one afternoon so you could see for yourself what I mean? And don't worry, we can sneak you in the back way so nobody will see you?" I think Lucy thought Fritz was losing his mind.

"Some more vermicelli, Fritz?" I said, desperately trying to change the subject.

"Fritz," Lucy said, looking him straight in the eye. "Who the hell needs to go out to see reruns of myself when I have every episode here in the den?" Then suddenly with the wide-eyed innocence and naiveté of a Hollywood newcomer, Lucy said, "Do they really watch me all day long?" We never did go to the gay bar but Fritz Friedman became a part of Lucy's small circle of friends and family who were welcome anytime at the house.

The next day we drove down to Palm Springs. Gary and his sister, Helen, drove in Gary's Rolls-Royce. Lucy drove Kum, Choo, and me in her Mercedes. I asked if I could drive but it was out of the question. "You drive too damn slow and you don't even know where you're going," Lucy said as we packed up the car. Kum and Choo giggled. I asked if we could take the champagne and caviar along that was in the refrigerator. "What the hell for?" Lucy asked incredulously. Before we left, I took them anyway and dropped them in my bag.

The two-hour trip to Palm Springs was fairly uneventful considering Lucy was behind the wheel. We did go a few miles out of our way when Lucy at first drove east along Sunset Boulevard instead of west to get to the freeway. "Aren't we going in the wrong direction?" I sheepishly asked. Lucy didn't say a word. She just slammed on the brakes, did a quick U-turn, and off we flew in the other direction.

Lucy's Rancho Mirage residence was a sprawling ranch style home located on the Thunderbird Golf Course. The house had a magnificent view of the course itself with the San Jacinto Mountains as a backdrop. On the drive down Lucy told me that Desi had won the lot that the house sits on in 1955 when he was playing poker one night at Thunderbird with Phil Harris and Buddy Rogers. At the time Rancho Mirage was much less fashionable than the nearby town of Palm Springs, which was already a popular celebrity mecca. But Desi instinctively knew a good investment when he saw it and he and Lucy settled there. Oddly enough, in the 1980s Thunderbird was still a restricted course and since Gary Morton was Jewish he was not welcome there even if Lucille Ball was his wife. Gary and other Jews—celebrated, rich, or both—played at nearby Tamarisk Country Club.

Lucy's next-door neighbor at Thunderbird was Ginger Rogers. Ginger was a distant cousin to Lucy, or so they both said, and it was Ginger's mother, Lela, who greatly helped cultivate Lucy's career when she was a budding actress at RKO. Lela was an acting and dance coach and one of the first people to recognize Lucy's comedic genius.

"I thought it's supposed to be hot in Palm Springs," I said, as I helped unload the car on our arrival.

"It's early, it'll warm up later," Lucy snapped back. "Besides, the pool is heated. Do you know how much it costs me to heat that damn pool? So you had better use it!" demanded Lucy.

"Yes, 'Mommie Dearest,'" I replied. "And I love you, 'Mommie Dearest.'"

Lucy knew the film very well, so without missing a beat, she said, "Then when you say 'I love you,' say it like you mean it." We both looked at each other and doubled over in laughter.

The weather did not warm up, not on that day anyway. In the middle of the afternoon the air temperature was about sixty-five degrees, and the water temperature about the same. I nearly froze my ass off when I jumped in the heated pool to take a swim. "Whoever you paid to warm up this pool ripped you off," I yelled to Lucy who I could see setting up the backgammon table in the living room. I stayed in the water just long enough to make Lucy happy and then went into the guestroom and changed into sweats.

The guestroom was actually Desi Jr.'s bedroom when he was growing up and I don't think there was any redecorating done since he left. The rest of the place, including Lucy and Gary's bedroom, was refurbished a few years earlier.

In fact I heard that the house had been redecorated twice in the last ten years. Paula Stewart told me that in the 1970s, as a birthday surprise for Lucy, Gary had the living room, kitchen, dining room, and master bedroom suite redone. New furniture, new drapes, new carpets, new wallpaper, new everything. When Lucy walked into the "new" house she went ballistic. She hated *everything* Gary had done. She ranted and raved so much that Gary stormed out, leaving Lucy alone in the house for the whole weekend. They did not talk to each other for weeks, and according to Paula it was the only time their marriage was in serious jeopardy. Eventually Lucy cooled down but not before she had most of what Gary did undone and re-redecorated the house her way.

Tom was flying in from Memphis later that day and I could not wait to see him. Lucy reluctantly let me pick him up in her new Chrysler LeBaron convertible, which she had just gotten a month earlier as an anniversary gift from Gary. It was white with a pine-colored wood panel running the length of both sides of the car. There were bucket seats in the front with a "dummy" stick shift in the middle. (The car had an automatic transmission—could you imagine Lucy driving a stick shift?) There was a very small backseat with barely enough room for one small adult or a couple of kids. The seats and interior were done in golden brown Mark Cross leather. The carpet was rich chocolate brown. The initial M for Morton was etched right below the handle to the door on the driver's side.

The car's oddest feature was an electronic voice that gave instructions like, "A door is ajar," when the door wasn't closed properly, and "Check your fuel," when it was low on gas. The "voice" was at first humorous but after a while got annoying. Lucy loved to talk back to the "voice." "A door is not a jar, a *jar* is a jar," was her favorite response, which she started saying a lot even when she wasn't in the car. Before Lucy gave me the keys to the convertible, she made me promise I would not put the top down. "You'll never get it up if you do, it's too difficult!" she barked. When I assured her I had no trouble getting it up, Lucy laughed out loud but still made me promise.

Of course as soon as I left the compound I put the top down. In all the excitement of picking Tom up at the airport and driving him back to the house I completely forgot to put the top back up before we arrived. And who was standing in the driveway anxiously awaiting our arrival. "Mommie Dearest" herself. "Oops," I said as I nervously and with great difficulty put the top back up while Lucy lovingly embraced Tom.

We played a ton of backgammon in the next few days. There was nowhere to walk and nothing else to do. And Lucy wasn't about to give me her car again. No matter what, we had a great time playing and looking at the breathtaking scenery.

That week the temperature never got much higher than seventy degrees in the afternoon, and at night it went into the low forties. And it was *so* dry. But every day Tom and I swam in the so-called heated pool to make "Joan" happy.

Lucy did not have many friends in Palm Springs and that was perfectly fine with her. When the phone rang it was usually Lew Rudin or Marvin Davis calling for Gary. Pat Stone, a close pal of Lucy's in Beverly Hills, had a townhouse in neigh-

boring Palm Desert and occasionally stopped by to play backgammon. Pat and her husband Charlie were avid tennis players
who were on the court for hours every day in the desert. Kum
and Choo brought down lots of food from Beverly Hills so
we dined out only once, on Thursday, their day off. We ate
in Dominick's, an Italian joint on the main drag, which like
Matteo's in Westwood and Patsy's in New York was a place
to sight senior celebrities.

As New Year's Eve approached, Tom and I wondered what
we were going to do. We were sure Lucy would accept either
the invitation she received from Bob Hope or Frank Sinatra,
who were both having New Year's Eve parties at their respective
homes. "Who the hell wants to go to Francis Albert's place?
Jeeeesus, what a bore! And I've seen enough of Hope, too," said
Lucy. "What do you boys want to do?" Lucy asked, like it really
mattered what *we* wanted to do. Lucy interrupted herself, "I
know, we'll go to Danny and Natalie Schwartz's house."

"Who the hell are Danny and Natalie Schwartz?" I snapped
back with my best Lucy impersonation. Danny Schwartz was a
guy from Queens, New York, who made good and now owned
Elmhurst Dairies. Natalie Schwartz made good marrying Danny
and they had an incredible showplace in Rancho Mirage.

Lucy was not wrong. Their desert home was magnificent.
The outdoor landscaping and the indoor furnishings were
magnificent. When we got there, for the first half-hour Natalie
kept looking at me like I was going to pocket some priceless
artifact from the coffee table. "Jesus, Lucy," I said, "Would
you give Natalie the 'high sign' or something so she knows
I'm not going to rip her off." They must have had some secret
desert code because after Lucy and Natalie made eye contact
Natalie finally took her eyes off me.

Cocktails and hors d'oeuvres were served from nine until

ten. Buffet supper followed with coffee and cake. I knew this was much too late an evening for Lucy and Gary so at eleven-thirty on New Year's Eve Lucy abruptly announced that we were leaving. She wanted to be home to watch the ball come down live on tape from Times Square with just her family. "Jeeesus, did you ever see such a boring bunch of wax works in your life?" Lucy kept repeating under her breath as we sped our way through the California desert to get Cinderella Ball home by the stroke of midnight. "Wax works" was Lucy's unkind description for older folks, women *and* men, who coifed their hair within an inch of its life and put on tons of makeup before they dared venture out of their homes. And although Lucy was seventy, and probably older than most of the wax works at the Schwartz's home that night, she sure looked a helluva lot better than anybody else.

"Next year we stay home!" Sergeant Morton ordered as her first New Year's resolution of 1982. We lifted our iced water glasses and we drank to our good fortune and then I toasted to how blessed we were to have Lucy in our lives. Then everybody went to bed except Tom and me, who in the cold desert moonlight, sipped the champagne and ate the caviar that I stowed away.

We left for New York City on New Year's Day despite Lucy's protestations that we stay a little while longer, like say to Easter. I was feeling very nostalgic for Manhattan where it was *supposed* to be cold in January. When we landed at Kennedy there was snow everywhere. People were jostling, the wind was howling, and the cab drivers were cursing one another. Ah, the wonders of the winter in New York. I was glad to be back. When we arrived at our apartment house the doorman handed us a Christmas gift from Lucy. It was a clock with a card that read, "You gave me the time of my life! Love Lucy."

Lucy & Snowmass

BACK IN NEW YORK LESS THAN A week and already I was missing Lucy. The novelty of sloshing through snow in the city was gone. But I was busy at the ad agency and I knew I wouldn't be able to get away anytime soon. So Lucy and I would talk every Saturday afternoon on the phone. Sometimes, for close to an hour, sometimes for only five minutes. It all depended on Lucy. If she answered the phone herself we would have a nice long chat. If Frank Gorey answered it usually meant Lucy was not in a good mood, and although he always put me through to Lucy, our conversation would be very brief.

In late February Wanda called my office and said that Lucy urgently needed to speak with me. The next thing I knew I was connected with the house. "What's the matter, what is it?" I immediately asked after I heard Lucy's baritone signature "Yes."

"What are you doing for Easter?" Lucy inquired matter-of-factly.

"*That's* what was so urgent? You know you scared the *hell* out of me," I stammered.

"Yeah, wasn't that a clever ruse to get you to take my phone call," Lucy said.

"Lucy, just for the record," I said, "If anybody tells me Lucille Ball is on the phone, I'll take the call."

"Anyway, so what are you doing for Easter?" Lucy asked again. Before I had a chance to answer she said, "Remember I told you about Snowmass, Colorado? I have a condo there. Actually I have three condos there: one was my mother's, one belongs to the kids, and one is mine. But DeDe's gone and Lucie and Desi don't go much anymore, and Gary hates it because there's no golf course and I hardly go since I fractured my right leg in four places ten years ago in a skiing accident. Did I ever tell you about that? Actually I wasn't even skiing, I was waiting to ski and some broad barreled right into me and screwed my leg into the slope. One day if you're good I'll let you touch it and you'll feel the pins and screws and bolts in there, anyway, whattaya say, do you want to go to Snowmass for Easter or not, I have to know, now."

"Okay," I said. With that Wanda got back on the line and gave me my itinerary for Snowmass in early April. Lucy had planned the trip and the travel arrangements even before the phone call was made.

Snowmass, Colorado, is a family resort community just outside Aspen about one hundred and twenty five miles west of Denver. In 1970 Lucy purchased, from architectural plans, three condos one on top of the other as a refuge for herself from the pressures and stress of doing her weekly series. Lucy loved the change of seasons, something she sorely missed living in Southern California. When Lucy, her mother, and the kids visited Snowmass in the autumn the leaves on the towering Aspens had turned vivid colors. When they used to go back in late winter and in early spring the snow fell as fast and furious as it did when Lucy was a kid living in Celoron, New York. Then in 1972 Lucy had the accident, and the kids grew tired of the place. After DeDe died in 1977, Lucy rarely visited Snowmass.

Tom and I were very excited about our trip. I was less excited about skiing. I had never skied in my life. I never had any desire to. So just like Lucy Ricardo would have done I lied to Lucy and told her I skied since I was a kid. I knew Lucy would be so happy that every morning we would be able to ski, right out from our back door of our condo, which sat near the base of Interlude, the intermediate slope. "Of course," Lucy said, "You'll take private lessons every day."

"Absolutely," I quickly replied.

This was the plan: Tom and I would fly to Denver where Frank Gorey would pick us up for the two-hour trip to Snowmass. Lucy, Frank, and Jeanine Foreman would get to Snowmass a couple of days earlier and set up the place with the help of Susan Whitney, the property manager, who delighted in assisting Lucy. Not in our plans was a ferocious spring snowstorm west of Chicago that closed practically every airport, including Denver's Stapleton. To make a long journey short, Tom and I got to Snowmass by flying to Los Angeles, then back to Salt Lake City, where we slept overnight on the airline terminal floor, and then finally the next morning we flew into Grand Junction, Colorado, where Frank picked us up. We arrived in Snowmass almost two days after we left New York.

It was well worth the trip. Snowmass, Colorado, was picture perfect. Having lived in New York City all my life I had never seen snow as white, sky as blue, or people as healthy. The skiers dotting the slopes looked like they were placed there by central casting. And all the "Beautiful People" who drank hot cocoa in hot tubs at the base of the slopes made me think that après-ski would be my forte.

Taking an investment tip from Desi, Lucy's choice in 1970

to invest in Snowmass real estate rather than in the more popular neighboring Aspen paid off handsomely. Just as her Rancho Mirage home appreciated faster than property in neighboring Palm Springs, the value of her condos skyrocketed during the next two decades as more and more people discovered Snowmass.

The interiors of Lucy's Snowmass condos were very much a replica of her Beverly Hills mansion. There was moss green shag carpeting throughout all three condos. Clubby upholstered chairs and ottomans filled the rooms along with some French Provincial furniture, which I heard Lucy had appropriated from the *Wildcat* set in New York and kept in storage for a decade. Lucy's "borrowing" furniture from a Broadway set did not surprise me in the least after our Westbury Hotel silverware heist. The kitchen appliances looked strikingly similar to the ones on the set of the Ricardo's Manhattan apartment. There were black rotary phones everywhere. Huge picture windows from Lucy's top floor duplex afforded her a bird's-eye view of the skiers who swooshed by her place from eight in the morning until the slopes closed at four o'clock in the afternoon. She especially loved to watch the little children—the "snow bunnies" in their multicolored parkas and pants as they tumbled and laughed down the slope.

Everybody knew when Lucy was back in town, and they would yell, "We love you, Lucy," as they skied by her place. When she stood on her balcony in her white-lynx walking coat waving like Eva Peron, many of the skiers in their excitement at spotting her would momentarily lose their concentration and take a spill right under her. She could never understand why so many people fell at the exact same spot.

While skiers were literally falling at Lucy's feet, I was falling everywhere. Before we arrived, Lucy had arranged private lessons with Twelvetrees, one of the best instructors at Snowmass Village. He went by last name only and he told us his aunt was a onetime film actress named Helen Twelvetrees, who committed suicide in 1958. Lucy's take on it was, "She was a drunk."

On our first morning in Snowmass we were outfitted for our skis. It took us forty-five minutes just to get them on. We were exhausted from our trip, and the thinness of the air at seven thousand feet in the Rockies made us breathe like we had emphysema.

Once up on our skis we headed for the hills. Regardless of what Lucy might have told him, it was obvious to Twelvetrees that I had never skied before. People were passing me left and right and they were walking. Still Twelvetrees suggested we bypass Fanny Hill, the beginner hill where most toddlers skied, and head straight to Interlude.

I have a slight fear of heights, which is not good for skiing. I wasn't too worried about getting to the top of the mountain because I had heard that the slopes at Snowmass had gondolas— enclosed cars, which took a bunch of people up all at once. I found out those lifts were on the more advanced runs. The lift going up and down Interlude was a traditional chair lift where two people sat side by side in an open-air seat with a pole between them with their feet dangling a hundred feet in the air.

On my first trip up the mountain I suggested that I ride with Tom. Twelvetreees and a precocious six-year-old girl cued up right behind us, and as I waited on line for the lift I noticed that the thing never fully stops to let people on and off. It slows down at the bottom of the slope and skiers hop on, and at the top of the mountain it slows down and skiers hop off. I was going to have trouble—I just knew it.

I was so freaked out about jumping on, that I dragged my ski along the ground and it fell off as we started our ascent.

Twelvetrees scooped it up while the little brat sitting next to him laughed at me. There was no way I was going to turn around in my seat and thank him. So with one ski on and one ski off there I was ascending the slope and too damn scared to enjoy the breathtaking scenery.

And then it happened. The thing stopped midway up the mountain. "Why are we stopping? Oh God, why are we stopping?" I was literally frozen with fear. "Oh God, why are we stopping?" Like a broken record, I repeated my mantra over and over as our chair swayed over the Rockies. It was my worst nightmare come true. After an hour (all right a minute) we started to move. When we reached the top of Interlude I skied off the lift with one ski. I guess I was slaloming. Meanwhile Tom disembarked and promptly fell down on all fours. The little girl was still laughing and beginning to really piss me off. She and Twelvetrees helped Tom up. It was a pathetic sight.

It took us just shy of three hours to get down Interlude, a run that would have taken less time to walk. But I was in no rush. And anyway, there was no way I was going up that lift a second time. By the second hour of inching our way down the mountain, sometimes on our skis, mostly on our asses I was beginning to get the hang of it. Twelvetrees was smart— he took us through some of the most remote sections of the trail, so as not to get us entwined with any other skier who had the right to be there in the first place.

Around four o'clock, as the ski slopes were closing for the day I finally swooshed by Lucy's place. I looked up, saw Lucy waving, fell on my keester, and slid into home.

I never felt so tired in my life. I could barely walk. That was it, no more skiing for me. I soaked in a hot tub alone, at home. Lucy vetoed my request to spend some time in the communal tub and outdoor café. Lucy and Tom played backgammon upstairs. I went to bed at eight o'clock and slept until ten the next morning. After a night of sleeping like a baby I decided the next day to be a grown up and give the slopes a second chance.

From the beginning, Jeanine Foreman decided, against Lucy's wishes that she did not need private lessons or for that matter, any skiing lessons at all. "The French Lady," as Lucy called her, said she had skied the Swiss Alps many times and she would have no problem navigating these slopes. On her first day out, before she even made it to the lift she lost control of her skis and crashed through a barrier. Her ankle was sprained so badly that the only powder she saw the rest of the week was the Epsom salts that she dissolved in water to bring down the swelling.

Lucy was very happy. With Jeanine's leg propped up on a chair, Lucy had a captive backgammon partner all day while Tom and I became enthusiastic if not great skiers. Unlike at the guesthouse on Roxbury Drive Lucy gave us kitchen privileges in our Snowmass condo, which meant we could brew coffee in the morning before we went out skiing. All solid food was to be consumed only in Lucy's apartment.

After we had eaten everything Lucy packed up from Beverly Hills, Tom suggested we get some fresh bluefish, steaks, and chicken for subsequent meals and he would chef our dinner every night. Tom is a terrific cook and he assured Lucy he knew his way around a kitchen better than around a slope. Still, Lucy lurked each evening in the shadows critiquing Tom's every culinary move, either to him or under her breath. He had to finally banish Lucy from the kitchen, sending her upstairs for a nap until dinner was served.

I was not so lucky in the kitchen. Lucy knew I wasn't a good cook because neither was she. I mean, look at what she did to franks and beans and she turned into the "Sixty Minute Gourmet" when it came time to fix a grilled cheese sandwich. Anyway, one afternoon when Tom was out shopping I decided to toast an English muffin for a tuna salad sandwich. I could *see* Lucy's eyes from the back of my head—she was so intently watching me split the muffin and pop it in the toaster. "If you don't how to make an English muffin, why the *hell* don't you ask for help?" Lucy muttered.

"What???" I asked incredulously. With that, she came into the kitchen, pushed me aside, pulled the muffin out of the toaster, threw it away and took another one from the refrigerator. At first I thought Lucy was clowning but she was dead serious. "You know what Lucy, I'm not hungry. I'm going downstairs." And I slammed the door shut behind me.

Unfortunately, this was Lucy's typical reaction when someone did something that she herself had trouble doing. She made a cause celebre out of something as mundane as toasting a piece of bread. It was unbecoming and unnecessary. Yes, there was no question about it—Lucy was a control freak who wanted dominion over every possible episode in her life, especially those she couldn't *possibly* control. I cooled off. Lucy buzzed the intercom a few minutes later and I came back up and we never talked about English muffins again.

Later in the week Susan Whitney stopped by and said she had arranged for all of us to go to Aspen that evening for a tour of the newly restored Hotel Jerome and Aspen Playhouse, followed by dinner in a local restaurant. "Lucy, we're going to a restaurant, that's a place where you eat in the same room with other people you don't know," I said.

"Don't be funny," she said.

It was a wonderful evening. Lucy got dressed up—no jogging suit and not a single hair roller in sight—and we were chauffeur-driven to Aspen in a white Rolls-Royce courtesy of the Hotel Jerome. We toured the hotel and then we walked through town to dinner. Afterward we took an open-air carriage ride back to the hotel. That night Lucy was as serene and happy as I had ever seen her.

For most of her adult life Lucy was a heavy smoker. In Snowmass she hardly smoked at all. The altitude made her short of breath, she said. So she smoked maybe one or two cigarettes a day. Lucy was also drinking less alcohol. When we were together in New York or Beverly Hills she would almost always have a bourbon or two before dinner. In Snowmass she stuck to iced tea.

In Aspen, I suggested to Lucy that she try a frozen margarita, made with tequila, triple sec, lime juice, and crushed iced blended together, which was one of the restaurant's specialty drinks. It came in an oversize goblet and she threw away the straw and drank it right from the glass with both hands cupped around it. After the first sip Lucy gave one of her "Vitametavegamin" facial and body spasms to the delight of everyone dining around her. She said the look of the drink reminded her of New York slush, so that night she nicknamed it a "slushy." That night she also convinced herself that a slushy was a nonalcoholic beverage, and it became her new drink of choice for the rest of her life.

After a slushy and a half in the restaurant Lucy à la Lucy Ricardo was doing her, "It's so tasty, too, tastes just like candy," and "Boy, it's hot in here!" routines. On the drive back to Snowmass, Lucy strongly suggested that I pick up the fixings for a slushy nightcap. Once home, Tom, Lucy, and I played backgammon late into the night sipping slushies and getting sloshed.

Lucy was feeling very nostalgic and she talked a lot about

the "Good Old Days" of Hollywood—of making movies with screen legends like Henry Fonda, Fred Astaire, William Holden, Eddie Cantor, and the Marx Brothers.

We were rapt. I would say, "Lucy, tell us a Spencer Tracy story."

"He was a drunk, but a brilliant actor. His concentration was second to none. Did I ever tell you Tom, you look a lot like Spencer?" Lucy continued, "When I first came out to Hollywood I did a movie with Tracy for Zanuck called *Bottoms Up*," Lucy fittingly lifted her glass as if to toast Spencer. "That Zanuck, Jeeesus, what a horror! Then I did *Without Love* with Tracy and Hepburn. Did you know that on the first day of shooting I filed for my first divorce from Desi, the one that didn't take."

Lucy ruefully laughed. "I was miserable and Kate and Spence didn't help. They formed their own cabal—they talked alone, they ate alone, they screwed alone. God, were Desi and I unhappy then."

I changed the subject: "Tell me a William Holden story."

"Well, he was a drunk but a brilliant actor . . ." And on she went about Bill Holden. Lucy talked about Carole Lombard. Before her untimely death in a plane crash Carole had been Lucy's closest friend and mentor. Lucy talked a lot about Carole and wept openly and unashamedly about how much she still missed her forty years later.

When Easter week was over and it was time to go home, everybody hated leaving Snowmass, especially Lucy. Before we left on our respective flights home Lucy made me promise that we would come back at least once a year. And I made Lucy promise that if we did, we would fly out to Los Angeles and go with her on the Learjet she leased whenever she went to Snowmass. "And don't forget the English muffins," I yelled as we drove off.

Promises were kept and we flew to Colorado several times over the next few years in Lucy's private Lear. I don't think Lucy ever knew how expensive it was to rent that plane—if she did, she probably would have driven to Snowmass.

On what was to be our final trip to Snowmass in late winter 1988, Lucy's overall health was beginning to decline. Trudy Arcudi, a highly respected Private Duty nurse, accompanied us to Snowmass. We nicknamed her TrudyArcudiPrivateDuty— all one word, and she was henceforward called only by that name. With TrudyArcudiPrivateDuty on one side, and an oxygen tank on the other, Lucy watched snow bunnies and me ski down her hill, and fall.

I had become a fairly decent skier over the years but she still insisted on having Twelvetrees by my side. She still drank a slushy every afternoon at five, which she insisted on making herself. I guess this way she could make sure how much "non-alcohol" she could mix in. And every evening after having dinner at home, we played backgammon while Trudy-ArcudiPrivateDuty knitted, and Lucy told tales of old Hollywood long into the night.

Lucy Joins the Army

I THINK IF YOU HAD ASKED LUCY whom she loved most in the entertainment industry she would have said Bob Hope. They did four pictures together— *Sorrowful Jones*, *Fancy Pants*, *The Facts of Life*, and *Critic's Choice*, and since the early fifties they each appeared on one another's television specials. Lucy adored working with Bob; she greatly respected his work ethic, his talent, and his friendship. In Lucy's eyes Bob Hope was the consummate showbiz professional.

Many of Lucy's appearances were on Bob Hope Birthday Celebration specials, which aired annually in the eighties when Hope was in his eighties and still working! I was lucky enough to be with Lucy on location for most of these shows where she was always billed as the "Special Guest Star." The show I most fondly and vividly remember was when I accompanied Lucy to Fayetteville, North Carolina, in the Spring of 1987 to work with Bob at Fort Bragg. Gary was playing in a golf tournament in Pebble Beach and Tom was busy at the office so Lucy enlisted my services when she "joined the army."

We flew first class from New York City into Raleigh, North Carolina, on Piedmont Airlines, and that's where first class ended. From Raleigh we took a one-class propeller "puddle jumper" into Fayetteville, and during the forty-five-minute flight Lucy signed autographs for the crew and all twenty-four passengers on board, mostly army personnel who were ecstatic over Lucy's trip to their base.

About Lucy and planes: There's a chapter in a Lucy biography that talks about how obnoxious Lucy was to airline personnel when she was flying. It goes on to say how she would not speak directly to flight attendants and if she ever *had* to, she was extremely rude to them. All this was "quoted" from an American Airlines spokesperson representing flight attendants.

From where I sat with Lucy on planes, which was usually right next to her or in the seat behind her, these tales could not have been further from the truth. Lucy did have a fear of flying and she was terribly claustrophobic. Takeoffs and landings were especially difficult for Lucy and she would grab hold of my hand so tight that sometimes her fingernails ripped into my skin. But as far as her behavior to airline employees was concerned, Lucy could not have been nicer or more accommodating. If we weren't playing backgammon she would chat with the flight attendants and when asked Lucy *always* signed autographs. When she left the plane she always thanked the crew for her safe journey. Sometimes she even complimented them on the delicious food, which I thought went too far.

The baggage claim area at the Fayetteville Airport was hysterical—army men in military garb picking up their duffel bags, while Lucy waited in her sable walking coat for her eight pieces of matching monogrammed Mark Cross luggage. There were no skycaps but it didn't matter. Lucy had a military escort as four enlisted men carried her bags to her waiting limousine.

We were driven to our hotel—the finest and nearest one to Fort Bragg—the Holiday Inn in greater downtown Fayetteville. The Holiday Inn had no doorman, let alone a bellman, so the limousine driver and I brought Lucy's bags into the lobby, which was jam-packed with army men and civilians who had heard Lucille Ball was coming to town. It was like *Best Foot Forward*, a movie Lucy made in 1944 where she played herself attending a military academy dance as a publicity stunt. It was bedlam. Lucy was mobbed every step of the way to the front desk. Fayettevillians had never seen a star up close and in person, let alone Lucy! Bob Hope was already in town but he was staying elsewhere. Brooke Shields, Phyllis Diller, and Don Johnson, who were also appearing on the show, were arriving later that evening.

The general manager of the Holiday Inn personally checked Lucy in and then escorted us to the "Lucille Ball Suite," named in her honor just hours earlier with plaque and all, and which was located on the second floor, the top floor of the Inn. The manager apologized profusely for having us take the stairs—the elevator was out of order and would not be fixed until the following day. The VIP Suite was two adjoining double rooms with a makeshift kitchen in Lucy's room that was thrown together by placing two bridge tables side by side with a coffee-maker and toaster oven on the top of them. Lucy thanked the general manager and generously tipped his assistant (all in one-dollar bills from her backgammon baggie), who went up and down the stairs five times retrieving our luggage.

When the hotel personnel were out of earshot, Lucy and I burst out laughing. What else could we do? There she was: Lucille Ball, Hollywood Royalty, sitting on a lumpy double bed in the Holiday Inn in Fayetteville, North Carolina, surrounded by steamer trunks and garment bags and no closets. The hotel room looked strikingly similar to the one the Ricardo's and the Mertz's shared somewhere in Ohio while on their automobile trip to the coast. You remember—the one with the trains that roared right outside their window and moved their beds from one side of the room to the other.

"Where the *hell* are the closets?" Lucy asked, quickly losing her sense of humor as she searched desperately for a place to hang her clothes. "And who decorated this place, anyway?"

"Tom Wells's dad," I shouted back from the adjoining room.

Lucy laughed. "Jeeesus, then call him up, tell him to hop a bus from Memphis and bring a closet with him. And when he gets here, tell him to fix the elevator, too!"

Lucy was completely thrown by the Touch-Tone phones in the room since she was so used to using rotary ones in her Beverly Hills and Palm Springs homes. "Jeeesus, how do I dial without breaking my nails?" She managed to call the front desk and get them to bring up portable clothing racks, which Lucy used to hang her gowns, slacks, blouses, and skirts.

"Hey Lucy, you could make a killing selling your clothes to the locals right from this room," I joked.

"You're not kidding. I could get more for this stuff than I'm getting from Hope," Lucy deadpanned back.

When the fun of unpacking wore off, Lucy and I rearranged our *kitchenette* and used one of the folding card tables for our traveling backgammon set to rest on. We sat on two of the most uncomfortable straight-back chairs we ever sat on and played backgammon for the rest of the afternoon. Later, Lucy wanted to take a nap and I wanted to scope out beautiful downtown Fayetteville. "Are you sure you want to go out? You might get lost," Lucy warned me.

"Get lost, *where?*" I said. Besides, I was getting hungry and thought Lucy would want to go out for dinner, so I wanted to see what was around.

What was I thinking? First of all, the restaurant pickings were slim and second of all, Lucy had no intention of going anywhere! When I suggested we go down to the hotel dining room for dinner, she said, "Nothing doing. We'll order room service."

Room service at the Holiday Inn Fayetteville was zanier than the Marx Brothers film *Room Service*, which Lucy had appeared in a half century earlier. After waiting for well over an hour, three busboys named Groucho, Harpo, and Chico brought up our dinner and fell all over themselves trying not to fall all over Lucy. The food was awful and it went into the hallway uneaten. I ran down to the nearby Piggly Wiggly and picked us up a barbecue chicken, a pound of mayonnaise salad that they called macaroni, and Lucy's favorite dessert, tapioca pudding. We ate dinner like there was no tomorrow on paper plates with plastic knives, forks, and spoons. And from the heartburn and indigestion Lucy and I experienced later that evening we weren't sure there would be a tomorrow.

At seven o'clock the next morning, with the Holiday Inn's uneaten meal festering in the hallway, we walked downstairs to meet the chauffeur who was taking Lucy to Fort Bragg. Like the day before, the lobby was packed with people eager to catch a glimpse of Lucy, Brooke Shields, Phyllis Diller, and Don Johnson, all of whom were now under one roof. "Jeeeesus, don't these people *ever* sleep?" Lucy asked, as she burrowed her way through the crowd. With no makeup or lipstick on, her hair tied in a babushka and with flashbulbs popping smack in her face, it was the first and only time I could remember Lucy refusing to sign autographs.

I came of draft age in the late 1960s during the Vietnam War. I was part of the first draft selection done by lottery, and my birthday, November 10, corresponded to a high enough number so as not to be called into duty. So when we arrived at Fort Bragg, this was my first time on an army base. Lucy had "served" her country during World War II by entertaining troops at Veterans' Hospitals from coast to coast.

There was an outdoor stage erected right in the middle of the base with hundreds of bleacher seats for the audience. Individual mobile trailers were used as dressing rooms for the stars of the show. Lucy's trailer was parked between Bob Hope's and Don Johnson's. As soon as we entered the trailer, Lucy, as was her wont, began rearranging everything for reasons known apparently only to Lucy. "C'mon, baby, let's go—get the backgammon board set up so we can start playing. And move these chairs around, and put the phone over there," Lucy ordered.

"Yes, General Ball," I dutifully replied, saluting Lucy. "Right away!"

That calmed her down. "Gee baby," she said, "I hope this won't be too dull for you just sitting here playing, waiting for me to rehearse. And *please*, whatever you do, don't leave my side." I told her it was a dirty job but *somebody* had to do it. We laughed.

The truth was that Lucy was a nervous wreck when she had to perform in front of an audience, especially when she wasn't on her own turf—that is, on a *Lucy* soundstage, where she was in *total* control of everything and everybody. Lucy worried excessively about how she looked, how she was photographed, the lighting, the sound, her singing, her dancing. She even anguished over her comedic talents. To ease some of the angst Lucy flew both Irma Kusely, her hairdresser from as far back as *I Love Lucy*, and Fred Williams, a makeup man from Desilu, in from Los Angeles to help her look her best. And I suppose I came along for, among other things, moral support and comic relief.

Before we could finish a game of backgammon, Bob Hope came in and wrapped his arms around Lucy and thanked her over and over again for coming. They chatted about the show and the duet they were going to do—a parody of "Yes, I remember it well" about all their appearances together on television and in the movies. When Bob left, beautiful teenage Brooke Shields came into the trailer with her mother to introduce herself. Then came Phyllis Diller. This was terrific. Hollywood stars, one by one coming in to pay homage to Lucy.

A production assistant stopped by with script and lyric changes and Lucy asked me to step in for Bob Hope for an impromptu rehearsal of song and dance right there in the trailer. It was like the classic *Lucy* episode when Lucy Ricardo dances with Van Johnson when his partner falls ill. This time I played the *Lucy* part and Lucy played Van, and no matter who played who it was wonderful.

Lunch was served at twelve hundred hours—noon— although Sergeant Morton would have ordered it for thirteen hundred hours. "Jeeesus, they eat so early around here!" Lucy groused. We ate cafeteria style in the commissary and Lucy said that army food was far better than what they served at the Holiday Inn. Lucy made me take home some rations in aluminum foil so we could have it for dinner that evening. After lunch we walked around the base, conversing with the soldiers, their wives and kids, with Lucy signing autographs and posing for pictures.

In the afternoon Bob and Lucy rehearsed their skit and song and then we went back to the trailer to pack up our backgammon board and head back to the hotel. We were about to leave when there was a knock on the door. "Miss Ball, may I come in? It's Don Johnson." Don Johnson at the time was white hot from his hugely popular television series *Miami Vice*.

He extended his hand to Lucy and she extended hers to him. "Hello, Don, so good to see you again. Don Johnson, this is Lee Tannen. Lee Tannen, Don Johnson."

"Hi Don," I said matter-of-factly but thinking, "Holy shit, I'm shaking hands with Don Johnson." He had a million-dollar smile that went with his million-dollar tan, which went with his million-dollar suit, that all went with his million-dollar salary.

Lucy had told me earlier in the day about her reluctance in meeting Don Johnson because she was sure that he and Desi Jr. had done drugs together in the 1970s. Lucy was known to make up stories now and then, so it was hard to tell whether she was telling the truth or just being a mother blaming somebody else for her son's predicament. "I don't want anything to do with that no good son of a bitch," Lucy said. But you never would have known it from her amiable chitchat and cordial demeanor.

We got back to the hotel at five o'clock in the afternoon and the lobby was empty except for a little girl about six years old dressed in a pink sequined tutu, pink tights, pink ballet slippers, and a pink rhinestone tiara on her head. She looked like she belonged in Lucy's all-pink Beverly Hills guesthouse bathroom. She was holding a dozen long stem red roses in one hand and an autograph book in the other. You couldn't miss her. She was sitting right in the middle of the lobby in one of the large upholstered wing chairs with her legs swinging in the air. There was a man standing on one side of her and a woman on the other.

As we walked through the lobby, the little beauty queen raced toward Lucy, scaring the hell out of her. "Oh, Miss Ball, Miss Ball, Miss Ball," she said, sounding like a cross between a Southern Shirley Temple, and Baby June from *Gypsy*. And

A family portrait, at Gary's sister Helen's son's wedding, circa 1968. My father is in the far upper right next to the centerpiece. Lucy's arm is around my eighty-six-year-old paternal grandpa, Max, who, when he was introduced to Lucy, asked her what she did for a living.

AUTHOR'S COLLECTION

Publicity shot for *Life with Lucy*, Lucy's final series, taken at Aaron Spelling's home in Beverly Hills on August 6, 1986, Lucy's seventy-fifth birthday.

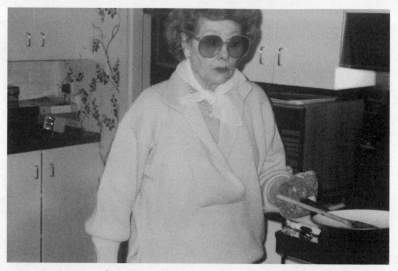

For Lucy, cooking was serious business. . . . AUTHOR'S COLLECTION

So was backgammon. (In this photo, doesn't
Lucy remind you of Harpo Marx?)
COURTESY OF PAT AND CHARLIE STONE

1000 N. Roxbury Drive, Beverly Hills 90210, Lucy's Beverly Hills mansion—my California home away from home in the 1980s. The guesthouse is center. Off to the right was Lucy's exercise room. In the background is the main house. It was paradise! AUTHOR'S COLLECTION

Lucy and Gary in Palm Springs, 1989. He could make her laugh!
AUTHOR'S COLLECTION

Lucy gets to taste "Hasty Pudding." (It's so tasty, too—just like candy!)
COURTESY OF TOM WELLS

Lucy with old friend Philip Morris and new friend
Charlie Stone at Obie's, the Stones' backgammon club
in Miami Beach where they first met when
Lucy was learning to play. Circa 1977.
(Lucy was over sixty-five and she still
looked sensational!)
COURTESY OF PAT AND CHARLIE STONE

Girls' night out in Beverly Hills: Pat Stone,
Lucy, and actress Ruta Lee. (You can bet
the backgammon board was nearby.)
COURTESY OF PAT AND CHARLIE STONE

Lucy's pool house in Beverly Hills,
circa 1986. Lucy's interior décor and
furnishings, circa 1955. (Notice the
eight-track tape deck and the rotary
phone sitting on the credenza and the
Lucy script on the coffee table.)
AUTHOR'S COLLECTION

The interior of the guesthouse
—with mahogany wood and
baby pictures of Lucy and Cur-
rier and Ives prints hanging on
the wall, it looked more like
Celoron, New York, than Beverly Hills, California.
AUTHOR'S COLLECTION

Lucy's personal assistant for more than twenty-five years, Wanda Clark, and me, on the terrace of my Manhattan apartment, 1991—I love Wanda!

Lucy and TrudyArcudiPrivateDuty at 1000 N. Roxbury on the way to the airport, on what was to be our last trip to Snowmass, March 1988. Lucy is telling TAPD that she didn't pack the trunk right!

Tom and Lucy boarding the Learjet in Santa
Monica for the final flight to Snowmass, March
1988. (Lucy was probably telling the pilot what
route to take!) AUTHOR'S COLLECTION

Lucy and me, Palm Springs, winter 1982
AUTHOR'S COLLECTION

Lucy and Tinker, Beverly Hills, summer 1982 AUTHOR'S COLLECTION

Lucy and Harvard "men" riding through Cambridge, Massachusetts, in the
Hasty Pudding Club Parade when Lucy was named Woman of the Year,
Saint Valentine's Day, 1988 COURTESY OF TOM WELLS

The *Mame* gallery in the Beverly Hills pool house. The space on the wall, lower left, became available when I took two photos home with me to New York. The photo just above and slightly to the right of the empty space is of Lucy and her mother, DeDe. AUTHOR'S COLLECTION

"You're my best girl." COURTESY OF FRITZ FRIEDMAN

Backgammon, Beverly Hills style: Thelma Orloff (left) and Gary Morton's sister Helen. (Thelma is happy: she must be winning.)
AUTHOR'S COLLECTION

Backgammon, Palm Springs style: Lucy, Tom, unidentified, Helen, and me. (I'm not happy about a move my partner has made.)
AUTHOR'S COLLECTION

Backgammon, Snowmass style: Tom and Lucy with the portable board.
(Lucy was happiest here.) AUTHOR'S COLLECTION

Lucy and me at the State Department dinner shortly after she was presented
with the Kennedy Center Honor, December 6, 1986, four days after Desi died.
(Lucy told me that receiving the Kennedy Center Honor was one of her
biggest thrills and the dinner at the State Department was one of
her worst meals.) AUTHOR'S COLLECTION

The four of us at the Ritz Carlton, Washington D.C., just before heading out to the White House cocktail party followed by the Kennedy Center Honors awards show and supper at the Kennedy Center, December 7, 1986. It was an emotionally charged weekend for Lucy, to say the least. AUTHOR'S COLLECTION

Susan Whitney, Lucy, and me bundled up in a horse and carriage on our tour of Aspen. AUTHOR'S COLLECTION

Lucy strikes a pose in the lobby of Aspen's historic Hotel Jerome. (Get a load of the Russian lynx jacket slung over her arm with her signature jogging suit and the Keds on her feet.) AUTHOR'S COLLECTION

Lucy, TrudyArcudiPrivateDuty, and me on the slopes of Snowmass in front of Lucy's condominiums AUTHOR'S COLLECTION

Tom Wells, Helen Maurer, Lucille Ball Morton, Gary Morton, and Paula
Stewart acting silly on New Year's Eve, 1988. Their headgear reminds me
of "Women from Mars," episode 89 of I Love Lucy.
AUTHOR'S COLLECTION

Poolside in Palm Springs, New Year's Day, 1989. It was
cold enough to wear the woolen sweater that Lucy
bought me for Christmas. AUTHOR'S COLLECTION

Lucy, Fritz's mom, and Fritz backstage after the final episode of Life with
Lucy was filmed in November 1986. (On the way home that evening, Gary
told Lucy her show had been canceled.) COURTESY OF FRITZ FRIEDMAN

Lucy's last car, a Chrysler LeBaron convertible with custom Mark Cross leather
interior that she got as an anniversary gift from Gary (I bought it from the estate
after Lucy died). The car now resides on Kauai where this photo was taken in
February 2001. Lucy loved Kauai and we never got the chance to go together.
(A door is ajar!) AUTHOR'S COLLECTION

Lucy and me in the last photograph of us, taken in Beverly Hills on March 11, 1989. Lucy died six weeks later, on April 26, 1989, at the age of seventy-seven.

COURTESY OF TOM WATSON

then she gave the dozen roses to Lucy. I thought, at any minute she was going to break into, "Let Me Entertain You."

"Why, thank you," Lucy said. The girl then told Lucy her name and said that last week she had won the "Little Miss Fayetteville Beauty Pageant." And in Lucy's honor she was wearing the exact same outfit she wore in the contest where she also won the talent competition, tap dancing to "Over the Rainbow." (What an odd song to tap dance to, I thought.) Then she pointed to the woman and said that she was her mom and the man was her talent and beauty contest booking agent.

Lucy was overwhelmed by the little girl's exuberance. She signed her autograph book. Then the little girl said, "Oh, Miss Ball, I want more than anything in the world to be famous. How can I be famous like you?"

Lucy responded, "You want to be famous like me? Well, with a mother, an agent, and a tiara, honey you are all set." The little girl started jumping around, squealing with delight as Lucy grabbed my arm and whispered, "Let's get the hell into our room and lock the door."

When we got in the room we saw dozens of photographs of Lucy that had been slipped under her hotel room door. Publicity shots of Lucy as a starlet at RKO. Photos from classic *I Love Lucy* shows. Pictures of Lucy from *Mame*. And they all had long lists of names and notes attached, asking Lucy to please autograph the pictures and then leave them at the front desk.

While Lucy was getting into her backgammon fatigues—jogging suit and furry slippers, I sifted through the pile of photos and came across a note from a private stationed at Fort Bragg with no picture attached. He said he was sorry for intruding on Lucy's privacy but he was writing on behalf of his mother. She had terminal cancer and she was too weak to leave the house to see Lucy in person in the hotel lobby as so many of her friends had earlier that day. He wrote that his mother worshiped Lucy and that for the last thirty years she kept trying, unsuccessfully, to dye her hair the same shade as Lucy's. He gave his mother's address and asked Lucy if when she went back to California she could autograph a color photo of herself and send it on to his mom.

Lucy was visibly moved when I read her the note. "Get her phone number from information, right now," Lucy ordered.

"Aye, aye Sergeant," I said. She didn't laugh. I got the phone number and Lucy dialed.

"God, I hate these damn newfangled Touch-Tone phones," she mumbled.

The private's mother answered and Lucy introduced herself. "This is Lucille Ball . . . Lucy, and I hope I'm not disturbing you." Evidently, the woman thought that one of her friends was pulling a prank, and it took Lucy a minute or two to convince her that she was the genuine article. Lucy found out that the woman and she were the same age, and that they each had a son and daughter, and that they were both originally from upstate New York. Lucy told her that not only was she going to send her a personalized autograph color shot of herself, but also a year's supply of henna rinse. Lucy told her to take good care of herself and to get well soon. Then Lucy hung up and went into the other room and cried.

That evening, as we sat and played backgammon and ate leftovers from lunch, more photos were slipped under the door and Lucy signed every photo before she went to sleep. I never saw Lucy as determined to acknowledge the love and adoration that her fans had for her. The next morning on our way to Fort Bragg for the dress rehearsal and taping, Lucy personally delivered the fan mail to the front desk with an admonition to the clerk that every one of the signed pictures should find its way back to its owner.

Both the dress rehearsal and show were taped before wildly enthusiastic audiences. The bleachers were filled to the rafters and there was no need for the Applause signs that dangled high above the stage. Nor was there any need for editing with a laugh track. The soldiers and civilians clapped and cheered long and loud every time an entertainer made an entrance or exit. They guffawed at everything Hope and Lucy said and did. The enlisted men cat-whistled at Brooke Shields while their wives and girlfriends swooned over Don Johnson. Phyllis Diller made everybody laugh, laughing at herself. Watching from the wings it looked like one of those USO wartime shows. Except the only "bombs" came from Hope's corny monologue.

There was a private party in the barracks immediately following the taping. Lucy as usual wanted to leave even before we arrived. One *shpilkas* from Lucy and we honorably discharged ourselves. On the way back to the hotel we spotted a Chinese restaurant from the limousine. Lucy decided that's where we *had* to eat. But it was late and the restaurant had just closed. Our driver went in, told them that Lucille Ball was hungry, and convinced them to open up. We had the restaurant to ourselves. Much to Lucy's surprise the lobster Cantonese and the egg foo yung, two of her favorite Chinese dishes, were quite good. The waiters spoke very little English. They just hummed the theme from I Love Lucy all through dinner and giggled a lot.

It had been a long day and Lucy was exhausted. The wig with all that netting that pulled her skin up gave her an awful headache. And her feet ached from the high-heeled pumps she wore all day. With the elevator still not repaired, we walked up the two flights of stairs to our room. And in her floor-length gown with her shoes in one hand and a container of leftover egg foo yung in the other, she looked like a coed at the end of prom night.

We checked out early the next morning with a whole pile of mail addressed to Miss Ball at the front desk waiting for Lucy. It was funny—in New York and Los Angeles everybody called Lucy, "Lucy." In Fayetteville, almost everybody called her Miss Ball. We were in a rush so I took all the letters and cards and stuffed them in my pockets. We flew back to New York via Washington, D.C., where we took the shuttle into LaGuardia.

Lucy was very tired so I started going through the mail, and came across this letter, which I handed to Lucy. She closed her eyes and told me to read it aloud to her.

Dear Miss Ball:

My mother told me that talking to you on the phone was the happiest day of her life. Sadly, I must report it was also the last day of her life. She died peacefully in her sleep in the middle of the night. There are no words for my family and I to adequately express our thanks and deep appreciation for your most kind gesture. We are holding a memorial service next week in Oneida, New York, my mother's hometown. If you could send the colored autographed picture of yourself like you promised my mom, we will proudly display it at the ceremony. My best wishes and God bless you.

It was signed with love by the private first class.

Lucy was stunned but she said nothing. She turned her head away, reclined in her seat, and just stared out the window until the plane landed one hour later.

Lucy & Life with Lucy

IN EARLY SPRING OF 1986, WITH Lucy and me still estranged, I read in the newspaper that she was considering coming back to television to star in a new weekly comedy series. I couldn't believe it. I figured it must have been publicity to counter the bad notices for *Stone Pillow*, but Lucy never sought or needed publicity.

I had not spoken with Wanda in almost a year and a half, since Lucy stopped speaking to me, and I missed her. I decided to give her a call at the office. Wanda seemed genuinely glad to hear from me and she confirmed that Lucy was indeed doing a new sitcom for Aaron Spelling Productions and ABC Television. I asked Wanda why Lucy, after saying time and time again that she would never do another series without Desi, Vivian, and Bill, that she could never top what they had, would want to go back to the grind of a weekly series. Wanda listened but didn't say much. Wanda always knew instinctively what to say and better still what *not* to say, and she said little else about Lucy or about the new show they were calling *Life with Lucy*. We chitchatted for a few minutes more and then Wanda thanked me for calling and said good-bye.

I then phoned Betty Cohen who filled me in on the rest. After *Stone Pillow* was televised and panned by the critics, Aaron

Spelling approached Gary and suggested that Lucy come back to television and do what she did best, a weekly comedy series. Aaron Spelling, who as a gangly young guy early in his short-lived acting career appeared in a bit part as a country bumpkin on an *I Love Lucy* episode featuring Tennessee Ernie Ford, was now one of the leading and most prolific producers of nighttime network television. At the time his empire included *Dynasty*, *Charlie's Angels*, and *The Love Boat*. (Later he would create and produce *Beverly Hills 90210* and *Melrose Place*.) When Gary approached Lucy on returning to television she said, "No way!" before he could even finish the sentence.

Spelling and ABC however were not taking no for an answer. Not before making their TV offer as attractive and lucrative as possible. They were so high on getting Lucy back on television that they gave the green light and top dollar to *Life with Lucy*, with a commitment of twenty-two half-hour shows without even filming a pilot. If Lucy accepted the offer, ABC would make Gary executive producer and pay him a large salary as well. I knew Gary well enough to know that when it came to big money, dollar signs would obscure the signs about what was or wasn't good for Lucy. But I knew Lucy better and she didn't give a damn about making more money—she had all she needed—so there was no way she'd agree to such a misguided venture.

Betty continued the story. Against Lucy's wishes, Gary made an end run around her and contacted Bob Carroll Jr. and Madelyn Pugh Martin and got a commitment from them to write the series. Then he went to Marc Daniels, who directed the first season of *I Love Lucy*, and he agreed to direct. Then Gary talked to Gale Gordon, the only costar still around from Lucy's last television series *Here's Lucy*, who said he would come back to work if Lucy said yes. Gary then presented the whole pack-

age to Lucy including Aaron Spelling's and his own partici-
pation, and when Lucy saw how much Gary wanted her to
do it, she reluctantly acquiesced.

I thought this was possibly the worst thing Lucy could have
done at this time in her life and wanted nothing more than
to tell her so. How I wished we were talking. I thought about
writing her again, as I had done a few times in the last year
but Betty said Lucy's decision to do the show was a fait ac-
compli, and she was coming soon to New York to do some
preproduction interviews.

A month later while we were working late one night, Tom
received a phone call at the office. It was from Lucy in her
New York apartment, and she was playing backgammon with
Betty Cohen. "Stop whatever you're doing and get your ass
over here, I want to see you!" Tom hesitated for a moment,
then Lucy continued. "And bring what's his name with you."

Betty Cohen and Lucy had become very close during our
estrangement, and I know Betty had a lot to do with getting
Lucy and me back together again. For this I will be eternally
grateful. That evening, on the way to Lucy's apartment Tom
and I stopped at P. J. Bernstein's delicatessen on Third Avenue
and picked up dinner for all of us, except Gary. He was in
town but he was going to Sammy's Roumanian on the Lower
East Side of Manhattan with his pal Lew Rudin.

As I was walking toward Lucy's apartment with franks and
beans, cornbeef, pastrami, and chopped liver, I was as scared
and excited as I was when I met her for the first time twenty-
five years earlier when I was a kid in the Bronx. Tom made
some excuse that he forgot something downstairs and so I rang
the doorbell alone and when it opened there was nobody there
to greet me. I walked into the living room and there was Betty
Cohen sitting at the backgammon table and smiling broadly.

Lucy appeared from behind the front door, slammed it shut, looked at me and said, "It's about time you showed up, now sit down and play." We hugged and kissed, ate delicatessen, and played backgammon and Lucy acted as if nothing had happened. At one point later in the evening Betty and Tom left the room leaving me alone with Lucy. I felt like I had to say *something*. "Lucy, I really want to apologize for what happened the—"

She cut me off fast, vehemently shaking the dice in the cup. "I *never* want to talk about it. Do you understand?" I didn't make any jokes because I *knew* she was dead serious. And I never did speak about what happened. In the end, our falling out and reconciliation was just like an *I Love Lucy* episode where Lucy and Ethel would have a fight and at the end of the show they would make up and everything would be fine again.

Lucy was very eager to tell me all about *Life with Lucy*, a little too eager I thought. As if the more she talked about the new series the more she would talk herself into believing she did the right thing. Of course, I made believe that I was hearing it for the first time. And I wouldn't dare tell her how I really felt. "Would you believe we're filming the series where we shot *Roman Scandals*? A million years later I'm back where I began."

"Yeah, but now you've got better legs," I said. Lucy blew me a kiss. I felt great.

She talked about how much she was looking forward to working with Gale Gordon and in the same breath said how much she still missed Vivian Vance, who died of cancer in 1979. In *Life with Lucy* she and Gale were going to play in-law grandparents who co-own a hardware store and work together. They also live together in the same house with their married children and young grandchildren. The series was going to be filmed in front of a studio audience on Thursday evenings as Lucy had done for twenty-five years. It would air on Saturday evenings on ABC, as hopefully stiff competition for NBC, which dominated the night with *The Golden Girls*. Lucy talked over and over about how glad she was to have some of the old writing and production gang back with her— sounding so insecure about her own abilities. It was obvious, to me anyway, that Lucy's air of excitement masked a palpable sense of despair that was heartrending.

All of a sudden Lucy changed the subject and started to talk about Desi. And then she started to cry. Lucy said he was diagnosed with lung cancer earlier in the year and had just a matter of months to live. Lucy talked nonstop, stuttering and stammering—first praising Desi's business acumen, then reviling his years of drinking and womanizing. But unlike the blasé way she spoke about Desi at the Brasserie Restaurant some years earlier, now there was a great deal of emotion attached to her words. She celebrated him professionally but cursed him personally. And the one thing that became crystal clear that night was that after not being married to Desi Arnaz for over twenty-five years, Lucy was still very much in love with him.

Lucy stayed in Manhattan for a couple of weeks doing lots of print and television interviews—as usual, hating the way she looked on camera and in the newspapers—and she attended the ABC affiliates convention and gala. Lucy was back in the TV spotlight, which was shining bright on her, yet was seemingly uncomfortable with all the attention. At the apartment she never spoke about the upcoming show. We just played backgammon, and every once in a while she would start to cry.

That summer, with Lucy back on the West Coast, we spoke on the phone almost daily, and as each preproduction week passed Lucy got more and more apprehensive about doing the show. She nicknamed the series "Life with Angst," and in many conversations she spoke about what troubled her most: Desi was too ill for her to seek his counsel and advice about the series. "You know baby," Lucy said, "He was the genius behind the show, not me. Nobody gave Desi the credit he deserved." I felt sorry for Lucy and angry with Gary for knowingly coercing her into doing something that was so obviously wrong. When I delicately suggested she bail out of doing the series altogether, Lucy's voice broke and she said, "It's too late now."

Filming began in the middle of July and Lucy wanted me out there for the first show. She was very nervous and I thought it would be better to stay nearby at the Beverly Hills Hotel rather than at the house. She asked me to come to rehearsals but I declined, saying I had some work I had to do. I didn't want to see what was going on until show night.

On Friday evening, July 18, 1986, fans lined up in the hot midday sun hours before they were let in to the bleachers built for Lucy's return to television, *Life with Lucy*. (Subsequent shows were shot on Thursday evenings.)

The VIP section was filled with family and friends like Thelma Orloff, Pat and Charlie Stone, Jeanine Foreman, Audrey Meadows, and Ruta Lee. I sat with Gary's sister, Helen, and her daughter, Randi.

Gary "warmed up" the audience as he had done for so many years on *The Lucy Show* and *Here's Lucy*. He introduced the cast one by one to enthusiastic applause. Gale Gordon came out second to last to a standing ovation. Then Lucy, not introduced, came from behind the show curtain, and all hell broke loose. The cast, crew, and studio audience burst into thunderous applause, whooping and hollering like they did when she took a bow from her seat on Broadway at the Palace Theatre.

Here was Lucy, "Live and in living color," as NBC used to say in the early days of the peacock network. With all her Lucy trademarks—tons of rouge and powder, the orange-pink wig with the skin pulled up under the netting, the false eyelashes out to there, and the ruby red lipstick from ear to ear. Lucy even wore her turquoise jogging suit, just like the one she wore at home. I'm sure Lucy wore it for luck. I hoped it would work.

Alas, there was no hope for the show. It was terrible. Absolutely awful, there was no other way to describe it. This show could not have been written by the same people who gave us some of television's most hysterical moments—Lucy drinking "Vitametavegamin," Lucy stuffing chocolates down her blouse from a conveyor belt gone amok, Lucy throwing a pie in Bill Holden's face at the Brown Derby, Lucy "soaking up local color," stomping (and wrestling) in a vat of grapes. But it was and yet they could not be entirely to blame.

Lucy was way too old for the antics they had her doing, which might have been funny if she was thirty years younger. Poor Gale Gordon just wasn't the foil that Vivian Vance had been for Lucy all those years. Everything was off—Lucy's all too familiar trademark gestures seemed tired and her legendary comic timing just wasn't there. Everybody in the cast yelled their lines, as if there was no amplification.

Of course, you never would have known anything was amiss if you were sitting in the bleachers that night. Whatever Lucy did made the audience roar. The laughter was so loud it sounded canned. Her every entrance and exit drew a prolonged round of applause.

The episode was filmed slightly out of sequence with the penultimate scene filmed last, which featured Lucy nearly setting fire to the hardware store and the fire department having to come in and hose down the entire place. Naturally Lucy gets caught in a tidal wave of sudsy water that floods the place, and she floats through the aisles wailing just like Lucy Ricardo would. But there was nothing funny about it. And not only wasn't it funny, it was so undignified for this legendary artist, to paraphrase Stephen Sondheim, to "be losing her timing this late in her career."

In the show's final scene she's back home apologizing to Gale Gordon and the rest of the family for being such a dunce. As I watched the scene I couldn't help but wonder if Lucy was apologizing to all of us as well.

Backstage after the show, Lucy was inundated with reporters and photographers, friends and family all wishing her well. She smiled bravely as she accepted congratulations. I stood back, off in a corner, and when Lucy caught my eye I gave her two thumbs up. She winked, mouthed, "I love you," and at that moment I knew she *knew* what a disaster the show had been. And there was no way to fix what was wrong because *everything* was wrong. What was Lucy going to do now?

I left the studio without seeing Lucy again, and went over to the house the next day. I was nervous about what I was going to say about the show. She was sitting alone at the backgammon table in the lanai, with her hair in rollers and little makeup on. The only thing left on from *Life with Lucy* was the jogging suit, which looked almost identical to the one she wore the night before. "Hey, what did you do, sleep in it?" I joked, kissing her hello.

"Who slept?" she shot back. Lucy begged me to stay another week, come to rehearsals and watch the filming of the second show. But I told her I had to get back to New York for business. I could have changed plans, as I so often had done in the past, but I had gotten a copy of the script for the second episode and it was even worse than the first.

We played lots of backgammon that day, and Lucy hardly talked about the show. She never asked me what I thought and I never told her. What would be the point?

The phone never stopped ringing. I never knew who called because Lucy instructed the staff that she wanted to talk to nobody except Gary, who was at an emergency production meeting with Aaron Spelling and the writers. Later, I found out that once production on *Life with Lucy* began, even Gary was smart enough to see that something was very wrong. He now wanted total approval of scripts and script changes, and Lucy's writers who never had much respect for Gary in the first place were making end runs around him and going straight to Lucy. The whole thing sounded like rearranging deck chairs on the *Titanic*.

Lucy was befuddled. Unlike the perfectionist she was in the "old days," she had neither the will nor the desire to fight anybody. So she agreed with everything the writers said, and did exactly what she was told, which was so totally unlike Lucy! Things at home became increasingly strained between Lucy and Gary as she began to see the writing on the wall, so to speak. I think all she really wanted was to quit the whole damn thing, never leave the house, and play backgammon all day.

Before I went back to New York Lucy made me promise I would return to Los Angeles for the television premiere of *Life with Lucy* in mid-September. By the time the first show aired, there were about a half a dozen shows already filmed—and from what I had heard, each was more disappointing than the one before.

When I returned in the middle of September I purposely arrived in Beverly Hills on Friday morning so I would not have to watch another episode being filmed. This time I stayed in the guesthouse. We played backgammon most of Saturday afternoon out by the pool and Lucy was more distracted than usual, looking at her watch every ten minutes. She said very little about the show and I could tell she was in a heightened state of anxiety, almost panic stricken about the premiere that evening. Lucie and Larry were in town so Lucy invited them to the house for dinner and to watch the show. When I suggested we have a little *Life with Lucy* party she looked at me like I had lost my mind.

Life with Lucy aired at eight o'clock in the evening, Eastern Standard Time, so just after five-thirty, Pacific Standard Time, Lucy's Beverly Hills phone started ringing off the wall. Lew Rudin called from New York. So did Paula Stewart and Betty Cohen as well as executives from ABC on the East Coast. Gary spoke to everyone, who of course raved about the show. Lucy and I played backgammon like mad and she pretended not to be eavesdropping on Gary's conversations. "Well Red, I think we've got another hit," Gary boasted after a dozen or so phone calls. Lucy rolled the dice and her eyes but didn't say a word.

Tom was in Memphis visiting his parents and I knew that after he watched the show he would call. So when the phone rang just after six-thirty in Beverly Hills we were sitting down to dinner. Lucy knew it was Tom so she answered, "Goldaper residence," and then thanked him for all the wonderful things he said about the show, and then she told him how she wished he was there with all of us. Then she hung up the phone and left the room.

At five minutes to eight, Gary turned on the big television in the lanai. That set was rarely on. We always watched TV on the little set next to the backgammon table or on the one next to the dining room table. As the sound and picture came up, there was a spot promoting the new series from America's Queen of Comedy, coming up next on ABC. "Oh wow," I said, "I didn't know that Carol Burnett is back on television." Lucy laughed for the first time all day. Everybody sat around the set like we were about to watch Neil Armstrong land on the moon or something. Everybody, that is except Lucy, who left the room. Gary shouted for her but she was off somewhere.

Life with Lucy began with a montage of clips from the first and subsequent shows. There was a shot of Lucy dancing by herself with headphones on while listening to music on a Walkman. There was Lucy neck high in sudsy water. Lucy flailing about in an out-of-control recliner. Lucy and Gale bickering. And clips of Lucy with her new television family.

Eydie Gorme sang the Life with Lucy theme. The theme song itself had become a bone of contention between Lucy and Lucie. Unsolicited from the producers of the show or from Gary and her mother, Lucie Arnaz had taken a shot and written the lyrics to a Lucy theme, collaborating with Cy Coleman who wrote the music. They made a demo recording, which Lucie played for me when she was in New York and which I thought was terrific. Ultimately Lucy and Gary passed on it and it was never used on the show. The new theme was not nearly as good and when Lucie heard it that evening for the first time you could tell she was clearly hurt by the rejection.

We all watched the show and laughed in all the right places. Especially Gary, who laughed the loudest. What else could we do? Halfway through the episode I looked around and saw Lucy way off at the other end of the room, sitting alone on a divan with her toy poodle, Tinker, in her arms. She looked shocked and bewildered. Did she think sitting farther away from the television screen would make things better? Maybe that way she wouldn't "see" things as they really were.

When the show was over, we all hugged and kissed Lucy telling her how terrific she looked and how proud we all were of her. Nobody actually talked about the show. The phone started ringing. Gary motioned to Lucy to take the call. She waved her hands back and forth and shook her head no. Gary took the call as Lucie and Larry said good night and left. Lucy said she was tired and wanted to go to sleep. I tried to kiss her good night but she gracefully maneuvered herself out of my way. She picked her beloved Tinker up in her arms as if the toy poodle was the only friend she had in the world. And not like the world's greatest star, but more like a world-weary old lady, Lucy climbed the stairs to her bedroom.

I went into the guesthouse, stared at the ceiling, and thought about Lucy—how she and television had been inexplicably bound for some thirty-five years, practically since the medium's inception. But that night the bond was broken and Lucy knew it. In more ways than one, it was the beginning of the end of life with Lucy on the small screen. And that night, in many ways, was the beginning of the end of Lucy's real life, too.

Critics from coast to coast panned *Life with Lucy*. Naturally, the first show won its time slot easily in the Neilsen ratings. Who did not want to watch Lucy? But as each new episode aired, the television audiences dwindled and in early November, after broadcasting eight shows, ABC did what no network had done since *I Love Lucy* premiered on October 15, 1951: they canceled Lucy. The series was performing so badly that the network was fearful that Lucy would bring down the rest of their Saturday night lineup with her. Five episodes of *Life with Lucy*, which were filmed, have never to this day been shown on network television.

On the night when what was to be the final *Life with Lucy* episode was being filmed, my friend Fritz Friedman's mom was in Los Angeles visiting from Boston and Fritz arranged to take her to see the show. Fritz told me that as soon as they arrived at the studio he overheard the crew saying that ABC was pulling the plug on the series and that this was going to be the last episode. He wondered if Lucy knew this and if she did know would she be in any mood to meet him and his mom backstage after the show as Wanda Clark had arranged?

Gary "warmed up" the audience and of course said nothing about the fate of the show. Lucy as usual came out before the cameras rolled to a thunderous standing ovation looking sensational and appearing happy. She spotted Fritz in the bleachers and blew him a kiss. The show ended and Wanda escorted Fritz and his mom backstage. On the way back Fritz heard more talk about the demise of the series. Fritz and his mom waited off in a corner while Lucy chatted with Aaron Spelling. "Fritz!" Lucy shrieked with delight when she noticed him and waved him and his mom over.

Introductions were made between Lucy and Mrs. Friedman and then Fritz asked if he could get a picture taken with Lucy, his mother, and himself. Lucy snapped her finger for a production assistant to snap the picture. "C'mon, Fritzie, you're a VP, PR man, arrange the shot," Lucy ordered, most likely for the benefit of his mother. Fritz naturally put Lucy in the middle.

The assistant was just about to take the photograph when Lucy snapped her finger again. "Hold it," Lucy barked. "Fritz, can I see you for a minute over there?" taking a firm grip of his arm and shooing him off. "Who's the important one in this picture, dear?" Lucy asked. Before Fritz could answer, Lucy answered for him, "I'll give you two hints, it's not me and it's definitely not you." Nothing else was said.

They walked back together with Fritz saving face in his

inimitable style—"What a funny story Lucy, of course I won't tell anybody." Then he nonchalantly rearranged the shot with his mama in the middle, and Fritz and Lucy on either side.

To say Lucy was devastated by the cancellation of *Life with Lucy* was the understatement of a career that spanned more than half a century. Fired from a job was something Lucy was just not. She prided herself on the fact that as an actress she had never been out of work since she came to Hollywood in 1933. Except once, she told me, she was unemployed for eighteen hours when she lost her Columbia contract and the very next day signed with RKO. And to be summarily dismissed from television, the medium that made her legendary was, I'm sure for Lucy, simply unbearable.

Lucy took to her bed for almost a week and took full responsibility for the show's and her demise. I remember how she would not take my calls, even on my birthday. I was afraid she was headed for a nervous breakdown. When Lucy and I finally did speak all she talked about was the failure of the show and that she and she alone was the problem. She repeated over and over, "I chose the writers, the directors, and costars. I approved the scripts. I made a fool of myself. And now all those people are out of work because of me." When Aaron Spelling tried to shoulder some of the blame Lucy wouldn't listen. When I tried to console her all Lucy could say was, "I wish you would have known me when I was really somebody." It was the most heartbreaking thing I ever heard Lucy say.

After the cancellation of her show the fan mail still poured in each week by the thousands, with generations of Lucyphiles still proclaiming their love and adoration. But she was convinced her fans didn't want her to work anymore. And as far as Lucy was concerned, without her work she had nothing.

Miss Ball Goes to Washington

AMID HER ESCALATING ANXIETY about *Life with Lucy* and Desi's rapidly deteriorating health, the summer of 1986 did however bring a bright spot into Lucy's life. The Kennedy Center for the Performing Arts announced that on December 6 it would be honoring Lucille Ball for a lifetime of achievements in the performing arts. The Kennedy Center Honors, then in its ninth year, was seen as the most prestigious American award bestowed upon people in the entertainment industry. In addition to Lucy, the 1986 laureates included Ray Charles, Hume Cronyn, Yehudi Menuhin, Jessica Tandy, and Antony Tudor. After reading about it in the *New York Times*, I immediately called Lucy to congratulate her. She said she was grateful for the honor, but ruefully added, "You know, baby, it should have been for me and *Desi*, just like they're going to do for Jessie and Hume."

"Now, you boys are going to need tuxedos for the White House," Lucy continued.

"What ever do you mean, Miss Ball?" I asked playfully, when in fact I couldn't believe that Lucy was inviting Tom and me for a weekend of celebration in Washington, D.C., in her honor. I told her I would have to check my schedule to see if I was free that weekend and then I abruptly hung up the phone. A minute later I called back to accept her invitation, but the housekeeper answered and said, "Miss Ball is busy at the moment, inviting guests to the White House. She'll get back to you in a few days." Lucy had gotten the better of me. A few hours later Western Union delivered a telegram addressed to Lucille Ball at 1000 North Roxbury Drive, Beverly Hills, California formally announcing our acceptance.

On December 2, 1986, four days before Lucy was to accept the Kennedy Center Honor, Desi Arnaz died in Del Mar, California. He was sixty-nine years old. Lucie Arnaz was at his bedside when he passed away. Privately, Lucy was grief stricken, almost inconsolable after she received word from her daughter. For the press her only comment was, "Desi was a great father, a great father." She never mentioned their personal or professional relationship. Lucy attended Desi's funeral exactly twenty-four hours before she left for Washington to receive the accolade she believed was meant for them both. It was a simple and private service, and Danny Thomas delivered the eulogy. Considering the vast television empire that Desi and Lucy created, there were surprisingly few celebrities in attendance at his funeral.

Tom and I arrived in Washington, D.C., by train on Friday afternoon, December 5. Gary and Lucy flew in later that evening, and we all stayed at the Ritz-Carlton. The scheduled events that weekend would include the formal presentation of the Kennedy Center Honors by President Reagan at the White House on Saturday at five o'clock, followed by a black-tie dinner at the State Department, hosted by the Secretary of State and Mrs. George Shultz. On Sunday morning there would be a brunch at the hotel hosted by Mr. and Mrs. George Stevens Jr., Mr. and Mrs. Nick Vanoff, and Mr. and Mrs. John Coleman. George Stevens Jr. and Nick Vanoff were the co-producers of the CBS television presentation of the Kennedy Center Honors and John Coleman owned the Ritz-Carlton in Washington, D.C. On Sunday evening at six o'clock there would be a reception at the White House hosted by President and Mrs. Reagan, followed by the Kennedy Center Honors (the television presentation taped for broadcast in late December) at the Opera House. Immediately following the show was a formal dinner for one thousand guests in the Grand Foyer.

Lucy and Gary finally checked in about eleven-thirty in the evening after a long weather delay. The world's most recognizable redhead walked into the Ritz looking absolutely sensational in black gabardine pants and black leather boots. Her flaming hair peeked out from the snow-flaked hood of her mink-lined, cocoa brown moiré raincoat. And when she caught my eye I ran to her like Patrick Dennis running to greet his Auntie Mame.

I was surprised at how happy and excited Lucy seemed. As soon as they checked in, the four of us went into the hotel lounge for drinks and a midnight supper. I ordered Lucy a slushy and she changed it to a Jack Daniel's on the rocks. That surprised me, because she had stopped drinking bourbon years ago.

Lucy was unusually garrulous that night, but neither Desi's name nor *Life with Lucy* came up in any conversations. We were all sidestepping those subjects. Around two in the morning and after two bourbons, Lucy finally brought up the cancellation. She was full of surprises that night. Lucy cursed Tom Shales of the *Washington Post* ("He better not cross my path while I'm in town!") for the most scathing review she had ever received, and then took Gary's hand and praised him for securing a one-hundred-thousand-dollar cancellation fee.

Although not privy to Lucy's contract, I knew that she had

received a great deal more. I asked, "What do you mean, one hundred thousand dollars?"

Gary nudged Lucy, "Honey, you mean a million dollars. ABC gave us a million dollars for canceling."

"Well, isn't that the same thing?" Lucy asked. She might have been tipsy but she *had* to know the difference. And then again, maybe she didn't.

Tom threw his two cents into the conversation. "You see, Lucy, here's the difference. A hundred thousand dollars is what I make for working all year. A million dollars is what you make for getting fired after thirteen weeks."

"So you see, Lucy, you should get fired more often!" I added. Lucy didn't laugh, and I suddenly realized that "fired" was a hot potato. Thinking fast, I said to Lucy, "This money thing reminds me of a story about a guy who goes into this bar at the Ritz and walks over to a woman and says, 'Excuse me ma'am, do you know the difference between a blow job and a chicken salad sandwich?' When the woman says she doesn't, he says, 'Well in that case, can I buy you lunch?' "

Lucy roared and shouted, "Here's to chicken salad sandwiches!" It was time to leave.

We didn't play backgammon much over the next couple of days. Lucy was busier than she thought she'd be, giving television and print interviews. Tom and I went sightseeing on Saturday afternoon and then changed into black tie and met Lucy and Gary in their suite at four o'clock. Lucy looked magnificent in a floor-length long-sleeved black gown beaded from the neck to the bodice. Irma Kusely, a Thelma Ritter ringer, was in Washington to coif her wig. And Fred Williams was there so Lucy would look her best. When she came out of her bedroom I said, "Lucy, you look like a million dollars."

Lucy winked. "You sure you don't mean a hundred thou?"

The Kennedy Center Honors were bestowed in an intimate ceremony with just the honorees and their guests along with invited press in attendance in the East Room of the White House. Tom and I were Lucy's only invited guests and I did find it odd but not surprising, considering the relationship she had with her kids, that Lucy would not want Lucie and Desi Jr. at her side when she received this highest of accolades. Or perhaps she did ask them to go and they turned down the invitation.

The President and Nancy Reagan presided. "It's no secret that Nancy and I have been friends of Lucy for years," the President said in an affectionate tribute, "and I think this redheaded bundle may be the finest comedienne ever." There was an ovation for Lucy. He continued, "Like millions of Americans, and people around the world, I *still* love Lucy." And then he added, "I know Miss Ball would want us to pay tribute to the man who produced *I Love Lucy*, and starred in it with her, the late Desi Arnaz." Now everyone stood for Lucy *and* Desi. I knew how happy those words made Lucy feel.

At the conclusion of the ceremony there was an hour-long cocktail reception, but Lucy got *shpilkas*, so we left for the State Department shortly after it began. Gary, Tom, and I made small talk in the limousine. Lucy said nothing. She sat right next to me but she might as well have been a million miles away.

Lucy perked up when we arrived at the State Department. There were celebrities everywhere. Bea Arthur, Glenn Close, Agnes DeMille, Jose Ferrer, Margot Fonteyn, Valerie Harper, Rosemary Harris, Quincy Jones, Walter Matthau, Liv Ullmann, Robert Stack, Hal Linden, Peter Ustinov, and Stevie Wonder were just some I remember seeing. It felt like Tom and I were the only ones there that we never heard of.

Seated at my table for dinner—I mean Lucy's table—were Lucy and Gary; Walter Matthau and his wife, Carol Saroyen

Matthau; Valerie Harper; Michelle Lee; Tom; and me. Before the first course was served legendary writer and director Garson Kanin toasted Lucy: "There are two ways in which to know a woman." He paused for a moment. "The *second* way is to direct her." Lucy's laugh rang out through the State Department.

The first course was a smoked trout mousse, followed by an entreé of quail pie with Umbrian vegetables, with chocolate cake and raspberries for dessert. "Jeeesus this menu is putting me into shock," Lucy muttered as each course was served.

"What in God's name are we eating?" asked Walter Matthau's wife, echoing Lucy's sentiment. "And what is this gray pigeon doing on my plate, and where is Umbria?"

Then I chimed in, "Right by Franistan," referring to the name of a fictional far-off city from an *I Love Lucy* episode

"How the *hell* did you remember that?" asked Lucy. (It was clear she didn't watch *Lucy* reruns.) Valerie Harper picked at everything on her plate—she was in her painfully thin period. Gary ate no dinner at all except for the chocolate cake with a Coca-Cola. Tom and I loved everything they served. Go figure.

Despite the cuisine Lucy had a ball at the State Department, and by the time she left she was as they say, feeling no pain. The three Jack Daniel's she had made the quail wash down easier, she said. "Now, where can I get something to eat at midnight in this town?" Lucy asked the limousine driver on the way back to the Ritz. And believe it or not, the driver found an all-night deli in some godforsaken neighborhood where I hopped out and got Lucy a white meat turkey sandwich on a kaiser roll with mayonnaise and a celery tonic. Which she consumed before we arrived at the hotel.

We got back after midnight and we were all beat except for Lucy who was raring to go. "Just a few games of backgammon for old times' sake," she kept saying. I had no idea what Lucy meant and I'm sure neither did she. Tom and I agreed and we changed into jeans, and went back to her suite. Lucy had changed out of her dress and into her Ritz robe but kept her wig and makeup on. She looked kind of spooky and was acting spookier. She was running around the suite like a whirling dervish, talking to herself and cleaning ashtrays and straightening magazines and rearranging everything she could get her hands on. Gary had gotten comfortable in a big club chair and Tom and I were sitting at the portable backgammon board ready to play.

When she finally stopped fussing and sat down she said, "God, it seems like only yesterday when I was with Roosevelt at the White House."

Without missing a beat I asked, "Which Roosevelt—Franklin or Teddy?"

Gary looked up from his magazine and laughed out loud. "Hey, Luce, that's funny," he said.

But I knew a split second after I had said it that I said the wrong thing. Lucy's whole face turned to flame. She started ranting, almost foaming at he mouth. "You think it's funny getting old. Just wait until you're old and nobody wants you around, and they throw awards at you because they know you're gonna die soon anyway. You think it's funny to lose your job and the people you love? You think it's funny when you can't do a goddamn thing for yourself anymore? Well, you can all go fuck yourselves!" Then she stormed into her bedroom and slammed the door behind her.

The silence that followed was deafening. After a minute or so Gary said, "I think you boys better go back to your room now. She'll be fine in the morning." But I didn't think so. As Yogi Berra said, "It was déjà vu all over again." And I thought about the year and a half when Lucy didn't speak to me, and could not believe that it might be happening all over again.

I felt horrible. It was a harmless little joke that at any other time Lucy would have found as amusing as we did, but not that night. Not after what she went through in the last month. This time I was sure I blew it with Lucy. So at three in the morning and sleepless in the capital, I was ready to start packing.

At four in the morning the phone rang and scared the hell out of me. I picked it up and Lucy said, "Where the *hell* are you? I've been sitting here at the backgammon table for an hour and a half waiting to play."

"Lucy, listen to me, I am *so* sorry for what I said. You know I would never hurt—

"Shut up and go to sleep." Click.

I woke up five hours later and felt like everything that had happened the night before was all a bad dream from eating too much quail. (Interpreted for *I Love Lucy* fans as, "A bad dream you'd have from eating too much Chinese food.") I turned on the television and CBS *Sunday Morning* was devoting its entire hour to the Kennedy Center Honors. Reporters asked Lucy about the award and she said, "This is the tops. It's even more meaningful because it's been such a tough month, with Desi's illness and death. I know we wouldn't have had as much as we have in television today, if it hadn't been for him." When she was questioned about whether she was angry over the cancellation of *Life with Lucy*, she said, "Noooo. Of course, it's upsetting, but that's different."

Walter Matthau, who was standing only a few feet away, smartly deflected any more questions by asking just loud enough for Lucy to hear, "Why does Lucy look so damn good?" Lucy winked, flashed a flirtatious smile, and walked on.

Lucy called our room later that morning and, thank God, acted as if nothing had happened. She suggested we skip brunch at the Ritz. She was definitely hungover. "Jeeeesus, just the thought of food makes me nauseous and who wants to see those same damn people all over again?" Lucy wasn't going to change her mind and I was going to be so agreeable that I think if Lucy had suggested we all jump into the Potomac I would have said, "Sounds like a great idea, meet you there in ten minutes." Her plan was more predictable. "Let's play backgammon."

"What a great idea." I cheerfully replied.

Lucy and I played backgammon for a couple of hours while Gary and Tom went downstairs to brunch. Lucy thought I seemed quiet. This was my one chance to go to the White House so I wasn't about to say anything more controversial than, "It's your roll," "great game," or "oh, what a beautiful morning."

After getting into black tie, Tom and I met Lucy and Gary in the lobby of the Ritz at four o'clock. All eyes were on Lucy as she stepped from the elevator in a burgundy high-collared (to hide the neck, of course) long-sleeved silk organza gown with matching belt, which tied about the waist and draped down one side. She wore the Kennedy Center Medal of Honor, which hung from her neck by a multicolored set of ribbons. She walked through the lobby and into her "carriage," like Cinderella going to the ball.

We were dropped off at the East Portico of the White House, where we were escorted through a metal detector by a Secret Service agent. We were then led to a sort of rotunda where we lined up within purple ropes and stanchions. There was a great deal more protocol than at the honors ceremony the night before.

Standing in front of us on line were Sigourney Weaver, Glenn Close, Pam Dawber, and her husband, Mark Harmon. With lots more luminaries in front of them. President and Mrs. Reagan were on the other end of the rotunda greeting each of their houseguests as they came through the receiving line. A magnificent Christmas tree with hundreds of twinkling white lights lit up the center of the room and the scent of evergreen in the air was everywhere.

The paparazzi was securely stationed behind metal barriers on each side of the room, photographing the guests as they were introduced to the Reagans. "Miss Jessica Tandy and Mr. Hume Cronyn." Flash. Snap. Pop. "Miss Beatrice Arthur." Flash. Snap. Pop. "Mr. and Mrs. Walter Cronkite." Flash. Snap. Pop.

Lucy was getting *shpilkas*. "Jeeeesus, what the hell is taking so long? You'd think Ronnie would know Wally by now," Lucy said, only half-kidding. Anyway, we were getting closer to the front of the line.

"Miss Pam Dawber and Mr. Mark Harmon." Flash. Snap. Pop.

"Miss Lucille Ball and Mr. Gary Morton." Flashbulbs pop, pop, popping all over the place. Shutters clicking at machine-gun speed. I was shaking. We were next. "Mr. Lee Tannen and Mr. Thomas Wells," announced the White House aide. There wasn't a sound. Not a snap crackle or pop. Zilch. Nada. Nothing. I looked around and saw photographers on their knees reloading film, changing flash units, and checking their watches. I was mortified. Then there was a flash. The official White House photographer took our picture with the President and Mrs. Reagan. A month later we received the autographed photograph in a black lacquer frame. It was our only proof that we were ever in the White House with Lucy.

The cocktail reception that followed the receiving line was an overcrowded affair. Lucy recognized few of her colleagues by face, and knew even fewer of them by name. She made me stand very close to her and when someone approached I would whisper in her ear, "Here comes Sigourney Weaver, that's Rosemary Harris, it's Edward Albee."

"So good to meet you, Sigourney," as Lucy offered her hand. "You look marvelous, Rosemary, what a gorgeous dress." "Oh, Mr. Albee, I love your work." Believe me, Lucy had no idea who Edward Albee was or if he worked at all! But Lucy was a master at making people think that she knew who they were. And everybody assumed since they knew who *she* was that she knew who they were right back.

I remember once escorting Lucy to an Emmy Awards rehearsal and Bronson Pinchot and Mark-Linn Baker spotted her as she sat in the darkened auditorium waiting to be called. Lucy loved their television show, *Perfect Strangers*. It was one of the few programs that Lucy watched regularly. So there they are running toward Lucy like two overly enthusiastic fans and I quickly whisper their names in her ear. "I know who they are," she snapped back. Of course, Lucy shakes Mark's hand and calls him Bronson, and shakes Bronson's hand and calls him Mark. I don't even think they noticed.

The Kennedy Center Honors telecast took place at the Opera House of the Kennedy Center, the largest of the theatres in the complex. Tom and I took our seats on the aisle in the fifth row just in front of Lena Horne. Lucy along with the rest of the honorees and their significant others sat in boxes on each side of the presidential box in the rear of the house. The format of the show consists of about a ten-minute film about the life and work of each honoree. Each segment is introduced and narrated by another celebrity, usually, a friend.

Walter Matthau took the stage to introduce the Lucy segment, the first of the evening. He recalled that the first time he thought Lucy would be a big star was when he realized that she was "Not just a tall, leggy showgirl but also a superb clown." The film rolled with clips from early movies like *Stage Door, Room Service,* and *The Big Street,* and later ones like *Yours, Mine and Ours, The Facts of Life,* and *Mame.*

Then Matthau talked about *I Love Lucy,* and we watched Lucy setting her putty nose on fire when she meets William Holden in Hollywood. And pretending that a hunk of cheddar cheese on an airplane was really her baby. And trying to get into Ricky's act. And trying to get into Ricky's act. And trying to get into Ricky's act. The laughter from the original soundtracks mixing with hysteria from two thousand fans in the Opera House was truly magical. I looked up at Lucy's box and it was the first time I ever saw her laughing at herself. The end of the montage brought everyone up on their feet to turn in her direction and salute this remarkable entertainer. Lucy stood at her chair, choked with emotion, and bowed to the adulation.

Then Robert Stack walked on stage and in a bittersweet moment noted that Desi Arnaz, who died earlier in the week, would have wanted to be there. He then read remarks that he said Desi Arnaz had written. "*I Love Lucy* had one mission—to make people laugh. Lucy was the show. Viv, Fred, and I were just props. And, oh yes, *I Love Lucy* was never just a title." Lucy could not hold back the tears that cascaded down her cheeks.

Dinner in the Grand Foyer was a festive affair. Joe Williams sang with Woody Herman's Orchestra and we dined on shrimp cocktail, aged filet of beef with mashed potatoes and roasted vegetables, and apple pie à la mode. Lucy was much happier with the menu then the night before, and I was happy I wouldn't have to search for any all-night delicatessens.

Our dinner companions' place cards included the CBS anchor Dan Rather and his wife, CBS chairman Laurence Tisch and his wife, and his brother Postmaster General Preston Robert Tisch and his wife. There was one more couple, a husband and wife, whom Lucy, Gary, Tom, and I didn't seem to know. Their place cards said Mr. and Mrs. Roger Smith, respectively. I figured that if they were seated at Lucy's table they had to be important. Of course, I'm sure everyone else at the table was wondering who the hell the two guys with Lucy were.

I was seated to Lucy's left and Mr. Smith to Lucy's right. Lucy desperately needed to know who he was before he sat down. After all, this was not going to be just a brief introduction, which Lucy had a flair for faking. Lucy would have to talk with this man all through dinner. Before I had a chance to find out his identity, he and his wife took their seats. Everybody at the table raised champagne flutes to toast Lucy and then the first course was served. Lucy turned her face in my direction and said through clenched teeth "What the *hell* am I going to say to this guy on my right? You've got to make small talk, and find out who he is or I'll kill you."

"I can't ask anybody now," I smilingly clenched back.

"Jeeeesus!" she said.

Over the shrimp cocktail Lucy turned to the "What's My Line" mystery guest and in one breath said, "Hello, Roger, I'm Lucy and isn't this shrimp cocktail delicious, and what do you do?" Subtle as ever.

"Yes the shrimp's very tasty and I'm Chairman of General Motors."

"Oh, that's a good job, too," said Lucy, without flinching.

Lucy Ricardo would have turned and given one of those wide open-mouthed grimaces. Lucille Ball just turned to me and made small talk but I knew she wanted to go through the floor, she was so embarrassed.

Roger and Lucy talked a lot over dinner, with Lucy admitting to him that none of the six cars that she and Gary owned was made by General Motors. By the time we got to dessert Roger told Lucy he'd send her one as a gift.

We got back to the Ritz after one in the morning and Tom and I called it a night—a night to remember. We had to catch an early morning shuttle back to New York and I didn't even jokingly want to say the "wrong" thing to Lucy after such an emotionally charged evening. I hugged her tighter than I ever had before and then we said good night and good-bye. "No good-byes, we never say good-bye," said Lucy. She then turned her back, raised her fingers high in the air, and waved. And then she was gone.

Lucy Goes to Harvard

" IT WAS VOTED IN 1762, THAT NO student should be an actor in, a spectator at, or anyway concerned in any stage-plays, interludes, or theatrical entertainments in the town of Cambridge or elsewhere, under the severest penalties." So wrote Harvard Historian Benjamin Peirce. However, in 1795, twenty-one junior classmates formed the Hasty Pudding Club, Harvard's newest secret society, whose constitution in part read, "Gentlemen, sociability is the source from whence flow the most delightful pleasures."

The Hasty Pudding Theatricals put on its first show in the winter of 1844. Continuing to the present, and still featuring men in drag, it is now the nation's oldest, and perhaps most original dramatic institution. Although women are now admitted into the Pudding and can accept backstage jobs, performing in the annual theatrical production is still an all-male proposition. Show business luminaries such as Jack Lemmon, Fred Gwynne, and lyricist Alan Jay Lerner, who wrote two Hasty Pudding Musicals, are counted as alumni.

In 1951, the Pudding instituted the "Woman of the Year" award to show its appreciation and love for women. Gertrude Lawrence (whose stepson was in that year's production, a farce called Buddha Knows Best) became the first of many remarkable women to pick up her pudding pot and accept the honor. Since then, "Woman of the Year" recipients have included Elizabeth Taylor, Meryl Streep, Ethel Merman, Julie Andrews, Katharine Hepburn, Ruby Keeler, Carol Channing, Roz Russell, and Ella Fitzgerald.

The "Man of the Year" award was established in 1967, and it is presented each year on the first night of the theatrical production. Johnny Carson, James Cagney, Steven Spielberg, Bill Cosby, and Bob Hope are just a few of its recipients over the last three decades. In 1973, a onetime "Person of the Year" was bestowed upon Gloria Steinem, who in accepting her award said, "This is one small step for mankind, and one big step for the Hasty Pudding Club." She then added, "I don't mind drag—women have been female impersonators for some time now."

Tom Wells was the president of the Hasty Pudding Theatricals in 1973, his senior year at Harvard. That year, Liza Minnelli who was at the height of her popularity, having received an Oscar for *Cabaret*, and an Emmy for *Liza with a Z*, was named "Woman of the Year." Her escort for the festivities was Desi Arnaz Jr., to whom she was briefly engaged. Jack Lemmon was "Man of the Year." When I met Tom seven years later he told me he remembered that the Club tried unsuccessfully to get Lucy to be "Woman of the Year" during his four-year tenure at Harvard. I told Tom I thought it was because she was busy doing *Lucy* shows, and had no time to come east during the winter.

Lucy was fascinated by Tom's Harvard education. She was an incredibly smart woman but with very little formal education of her own. At barely fifteen years of age she quit high school in Jamestown, New York, to enroll in drama school in Manhattan. It was the Robert Minton-John Murray Anderson

School of Drama, on East Fifty-eighth Street, where Bette Davis was then the star pupil. After only one month the school wrote her mother, DeDe, that she was wasting her money—Lucy would never be a good actress—and Lucy went back home.

"What was it like going to an Ivy League college? And how the hell did you have time to study, learn Latin, and do those wonderful shows?" Lucy would ask Tom on more than one occasion.

From 1980, I decided to make it my mission to get Lucy to be Hasty Pudding's "Woman of the Year." Every year, I'd ask her and every year she'd turn me down, even though she wasn't working and just filling her days mostly playing back-gammon. "Why the hell would they want me?" I kept pushing. She kept pulling back. And after the *Life with Lucy* fiasco in 1986 I didn't think we would ever get the clown of the century to be the "Woman of the Year."

One day in the fall of 1987 Lucy called and asked, "How do I get into Harvard?"

"Practice," I shot back, like the answer to the old, "How do I get to Carnegie Hall" riddle. The "Woman of the Year" celebration traditionally took place in mid-February, while the Hasty Pudding show was in rehearsal. Tom immediately set the wheels in motion, and a few weeks later the press announced that Lucille Ball was named Hasty Pudding's 1988 "Woman of the Year." Lucy herself was amazed at how much attention the award generated and she became more and more excited about her upcoming visit to the Cambridge, Massachusetts, campus. But I don't think she had any idea about how the magnitude of her appearance would change the college town.

Beginning in 1973, when Liza Minnelli was "Woman of the Year," honorees have been treated to a parade through the streets of Cambridge. They ride in a convertible alongside the stars of the show, who don full drag for the occasion. Jugglers, acrobats, unicyclists, and fire engines trail the parade route.

Lucy arrived at Harvard on Valentine's Day, 1988, and Cambridge, Massachusetts, gave the royal treatment to the still reigning "Queen of Comedy." Newspapers from coast to coast, *Time, Newsweek,* and the lead story on *Entertainment Tonight* that night reported that the turnout for the Pudding parade through Harvard Square was by far the largest in its history. Thousands of fans braved the bitter cold to cheer Lucy along the route, where she rode on the trunk of the convertible flanked by two burly Harvard men in fabulous wigs and dresses. Lucy herself looked smashing in a white Russian-lynx coat and matching muff, which she held high above her head and used to wave to the crowd. Lucy was ecstatic, happier than I had seen her in a long, long time.

After the parade we went back to the Charles Hotel where Lucy, Gary, Tom, and I shared a three-bedroom suite for our two-night stay in Cambridge. Lucy was physically exhausted but emotionally energized from all the afternoon's excitement. The adoration she received that day was just what a doctor would have ordered to get her out of the funk she'd been in since Desi's death and the failure of her show. We played some backgammon and then Lucy took a nap. Tom and I headed to the clubhouse where Lucy would receive the "Woman of the Year" Hasty Pudding Pot on stage. Unbeknownst to Lucy, we arranged for her to actually taste "Hasty Pudding"—a nasty concoction of milk, molasses, cornmeal, nutmeg, butter, and salt. We knew Lucy would play it to the hilt and the press was sure to have a great photo opportunity.

The Pudding Theatre was standing room only. After a brief introduction, Lucy was called on stage and the audience went wild. She graciously bowed and wiped tears from her eyes. She was genuinely touched by the adoration of these young fans, none of whom were even born when *I Love Lucy* first went on the air in 1951.

Before bestowing the award on her, the stars of the show told Lucy they had a special surprise for her. Lucy gave that, "I'm in for it" look to the audience, and they already began to laugh. "Miss Ball, all of us at the Hasty Pudding Theatricals would be honored if you would taste our recipe for Hasty Pudding and tell us if it meets your high standards of culinary artistry." They gave Lucy a spoonful of pudding and she swallowed it down. It was "Vitametavegamin" all over again. A look of disgust crossed her face, her mouth began contorting, her eyes started crossing, her upper body went into spasms that were as funny and priceless as they were thirty-five years earlier. And Lucy *looked* decades younger, as if she were actually reliving some wonderful, magical timeless moment of her life. The kids and faculty were hysterical. The photographers were having a field day, and Lucy was on top of her game and on top of the world. She refused to give the Hasty Pudding back and every so often during the awards presentation she took a swig, just for laughs.

That evening's dinner was a black-tie affair in the dining room of the Hasty Pudding Club on Holyoke Street. Lucy and Gary sat on the dais along with the producers of the Hasty Pudding Theatricals, the stars of the show, and Tom and me. Lucy was feted in grand style with lots of toasts. Just about everyone in the dining hall had something wonderful to say about Lucy and she was deeply moved by the occasion. When it was Lucy's turn to speak, she said, "I hope all of you young, beautiful, and talented people have as much happiness in your whole life as you have given me this evening."

The next day Gary invited a small group of Harvard undergraduates who were interested in pursuing a theatrical career to meet Lucy at the hotel for a question and answer session about her life and her work. It was a wonderful hour, one in which Lucy wound up lecturing the young people on the value of a good education even if they wanted to break into show business. "Always have something to fall back on, but if you want to be in show business, give it everything you got. And for God's sake, do *anything* anybody asks of you. Take *any* part, take *any* pratfall and learn it all."

One of the students asked, "You became such a big star. How much do you think was talent and how much was luck?"

Lucy chuckled, "Let's put it this way. I got kicked out of drama school. They fired me when I was a waitress because I forgot to put the banana in the banana split. I couldn't sing. I couldn't dance. What else could I do? I had to be a star." Then she hugged each and every one of them and said, "Now get the hell out of here and go change the world."

Lucy & the Massage Therapist

IN THE SPRING OF 1988, LUCY guest-starred in a two-hour NBC tribute to Bob Hope. Throughout the decade, Lucy had appeared on various birthday celebrations like the one she did at Fort Bragg. Whenever Bob called, Lucy was there, although this time she was very reluctant to do the show. Lucy was in a serious depression. Except for the trip to Harvard and a visit to Snowmass earlier in the year, Lucy stayed behind the closed shutters of her Beverly Hills lanai playing backgammon mostly with her sister-in-law, Helen, Thelma Orloff, and a new backgammon pal, a writer named Jim Brochu. She and Gary rarely went out to dinner. Even when the help was off, Lucy preferred eating leftovers at home. She was in near constant pain from her shoulder. She was having problems with her gums, and according to Lucy, her "plumbing" wasn't working the way it was supposed to. She talked a lot about being fired from television and a lot about Vivian Vance. She was very nostalgic. And she cried a lot.

After much cajoling from everyone around her, Lucy agreed to make a cameo appearance on the Hope show and just chat with Bob about old times while they ran film clips. The producers had something else in mind and they convinced Lucy to sing and dance to an original song called "Comedy Is a Serious Business," with a group of gypsies (dancers) backing her up. Lucy would have a week of rehearsal and then the show would be taped in front of an invited audience, made up mostly of entertainers who worked with Bob over the years. She finally agreed and each night after rehearsal, I called Lucy to see how things were going. I had hoped being "back on her feet" would boost her spirits, but Lucy was blasé at best about the work and said she was exhausted and terrified at the prospect of performing in front of an audience, especially of her peers. "But that's what you do best," I said.

"Not anymore," Lucy answered.

On show night, at nearly seventy-six years old, Lucy walked out on stage in a double-breasted black tuxedo jacket, black leotards, and black high-heeled pumps to a standing ovation. She looked terrific. The star-studded audience applauded her every move as if they knew she needed their adoration more than ever. I watched the show at home in New York and although I could see that Lucy was scared out of her wits she did a great job. I was so proud of her and I prayed that when Lucy saw how great she looked on camera and how much the audience loved her it would give her a new lease on life.

A couple of days after the show was aired in early May, Lucy suffered a stroke, and Gary rushed her to Cedars-Sinai Medical Center in Los Angeles by himself. After spending less than twenty-four hours in intensive care, Lucy demanded to go home and she was released from the hospital soon after. TrudyArcudiPrivateDuty moved into Lucie's old room on Roxbury Drive and took terrific care of Lucy.

I didn't ask anybody, I just decided to fly out and surprise Lucy on Mother's Day. Lucy's favorite flower was lilac, which you could not find on the West Coast, so I filled an industrial-size Hefty garbage bag with lilacs and brought them with me on the plane to Los Angeles. Coach class never smelled so sweet.

When I arrived, the housekeeper let me in and I climbed the stairs to Lucy's room. Oh, God, I thought, What if Lucy sees me and has another stroke. She was propped up in bed facing away from me with TrudyArcudiPrivateDuty at her bedside. Without a word, I spread the lilacs all over the bed. She looked up at me and I jumped into bed, got under the covers and told Lucy that I wasn't leaving until she got better.

With no makeup on and her unwashed hair slicked back from her forehead, Lucy was barely recognizable. "You look great," I lied. "Strokes agree with you."

"You're full of shit," she shot back. Her mouth was slightly crooked, and a bit of saliva trickled out from one side. And she had trouble raising her left arm. We played backgammon in bed for an hour or so, the board on top of a breakfast tray between Lucy and me and the lilacs spread all around us.

After Lucy fell asleep TrudyArcudiPrivateDuty told me the doctors said it was not a major stroke and they expected her to make a full recovery. They thought she overexerted herself doing the Hope show. In time, they said, her mouth would straighten out and her slurred speech and slightly paralyzed left side would return to normal.

I took some vacation time and I stayed with Lucy for the next couple of weeks. She got stronger each day. Although she slept a great deal of the time Lucy and I did manage to get in an hour or two of backgammon each day. Jim Brochu and I had fun pretending to be jealous of each other, as we vied for Lucy's attention, and Lucy loved every minute of it. And she made me wake her up so she could watch Oprah Winfrey every afternoon. Lucy was crazy about Oprah, very early on, before Oprah's meteoric rise in popularity. Lucy's pal Onna White, who choreographed *Mame*, came by the house almost daily to help Lucy regain the use of her arms and legs. They also worked together on getting Lucy's speech back. TrudyArcudiPrivateDuty (TAPD) suggested to Lucy that she add massage therapy to her daily physical regimen. Lucy was not crazy about the idea, but the good nurse called an Israeli gentleman named Ahmos Netanel and told him to bring his massage table to the house on Roxbury Drive.

Lucy was always very wary of new people in her home, especially an employee whom she had not personally interviewed. But TAPD assured Lucy that Ahmos was first rate and that she had known him since she was the private duty nurse for Nora Kaye, the prima ballerina turned choreographer who was married to director Herbert Ross. Ahmos had given daily massage therapy treatments to Nora at her home, which helped to greatly ease her pain. In fact Lucy and I were playing backgammon when TAPD mentioned Ahmos's name for the first time. She told us that Nora Kaye was so grateful to those who cared for her during the last months of her life that in her will she bequeathed one hundred thousand dollars to be divided among the staff. Trudy had hoped that Ahmos was included in her generosity. Lucy didn't say a word. Then Trudy repeated, "Can you imagine, one hundred thousand dollars to the *staff*?"

There was complete silence for a minute or so. Finally, I couldn't resist. "Well, TrudyArcudiPrivateDuty, *that* was subtle," I finally said. Then we all broke up.

Lucy told TAPD that when she called Ahmos she was to tell him to come over to Mrs. Morton's home, not Lucille Ball's, and then give him only the address not the phone number. "When he arrives," Lucy said, "I will talk to him and tell him what he needs to do." Oh, this should be priceless, I thought, Lucy's going to tell Ahmos how to give a massage.

Later that afternoon, Ahmos arrived, massage table in hand. Lucy told him to follow her upstairs to her bedroom. An hour later Ahmos came downstairs to the lanai. "Mrs. Morton is one tough cracker," Ahmos said, speaking with a heavy Israeli accent. He said she told him to come back the next morning at ten.

Lucy was very embarrassed by her debilitations, so she begged Ahmos to keep her condition confidential; in fact, she made him promise he would not tell anybody that he was giving her daily physiotherapy. Lucy grew fond of Ahmos very quickly and soon he was spending a couple of hours each day giving Lucy massage therapy and doing stretching and flexibility exercises with her. At the end of each session, he came downstairs and reported on her prognosis. Ahmos told me he was puzzled by one thing—every time he asked Lucy to walk around the block for exercise, she would say, "No way, I can't, there are tourists." And then she would change the subject. Every day he made the same suggestion and everyday he got the same response. Sometimes he would just repeat "Tourists?" and she would say, "Yeah, tourists!" I said nothing, not wanting to get involved, also knowing how sensitive Lucy was at being seen in public not looking her best.

Finally, Ahmos would not take "Tourists" for an answer and he told Lucy that the next morning he would pick her up at the house and they would take a brisk walk around the block. Lucy reluctantly agreed and the following day she put on her white jogging suit and sneakers, and tied a scarf around her head and right after breakfast off they went. Five minutes later they came back. Lucy was furious. She went upstairs and slammed her bedroom door shut.

Ahmos came into Gary's den where I was having breakfast. "What happened?" I asked. Ahmos told me that no sooner had they walked fifty feet from the house, tour buses and cars came to screeching halts and people began yelling, "We love you, Lucy, you're the greatest, get well soon."

Then Lucy angrily said, "I told you about the tourists, now do you believe me?" Then she dug her fingernails into his arm and pulled him home.

I explained to Ahmos that ordinarily Lucy did not mind being recognized and acknowledged, but because of her impairments she was very self-conscious about going out in public. So instead of feeling good about the adoration she was receiving she got embarrassed and angry. "I don't understand, Lee, why does *everybody* in the neighborhood seem to know Mrs. Morton?" Ahmos asked, surprised by all the attention she received.

"What do you mean, Ahmos, you wonder why everybody knows her?" I stared at him in amazement. "Don't *you* know who Mrs. Morton is?"

He smiled at me and said, "I know she's very rich, and sometimes she's funny," he said.

"Sit down, Ahmos, I've got something to tell you."

When I told Ahmos who Mrs. Morton was he still didn't know what I was talking about. Here's the story, unbelievable but true: Ahmos Netanel was probably in his middle twenties. He grew up on a kibbutz in Israel where he watched no American television. After high school, like all other Israeli men and women his age, he joined the army and served his country for three years. When he got out of the military he came to live in Southern California with his sister who had immigrated to the United States some years earlier. He studied massage therapy and worked long hours to hone his craft and build his practice, which had started to include sports and enter-tainment celebrities. Other than the late news he had no time to watch television. When TrudyArcudiPrivateDuty invited him to work for Mrs. Morton he assumed she was another rich Beverly Hills matron who could well afford his services on a daily basis. And when Lucy asked him to keep their relationship a secret, he never mentioned her name to any-body.

Rather than talk any more about Lucy, who was still upstairs in her room, I pulled out a video and Ahmos watched his first *I Love Lucy*, and I watched Ahmos watching Lucy, which was almost as funny as the show.

At the end of the show he was blown away. "This cannot be the same woman, it is impossible," he kept repeating. I assured him it was, although I agreed with him and told him that at times I still had trouble believing that it was the same woman in real life that was on the TV screen. Ahmos never told Mrs. Morton he knew who she really was, and surpris-ingly enough, the very next day Lucy suggested they take an-other walk. When people shouted out to her Ahmos made believe he didn't hear a word they said. And to the day she died Lucy's massage therapist never told her he knew who she really was.

Last Laughs: 1989

WE USHERED IN 1989 IN PALM Springs, California, in true Lucy style—staying home and playing games on New Year's Eve. The guest list was Gary and his sister, Helen, Paula Stewart, Tom, Lucy, and me. After our outing to Danny and Natalie Schwartz with the wax works a few years earlier, Lucy swore she would never again go out on December 31. Besides, this Christmas season Lucy was in anything but a jolly mood. She was more reclusive and depressed than I'd ever seen her. And she still felt ill at ease about going out in public since her stroke six months earlier, which still left her with a slight speech impediment and a crooked bottom lip.

Lucy was also very upset about *The Richard Burton Diaries*, a recently published book in which Burton was quoted as saying that after he and Elizabeth Taylor did a *Here's Lucy* show he swore he would never work with Lucy again. We all knew how devastated Lucy would be to learn how Burton felt, so we tried, unsuccessfully, to keep the book out of her hands. Celebrity bios were Lucy's favorite, so it wasn't long before she read the terrible things he had to say about her in print. Lucy read about how impossible he thought she was on the set—bossy, giving him and everyone else line readings, suggesting he shout every piece of dialogue at the top of his lungs, and on and on. In one pernicious journal entry, on the day the episode was filmed, Lucy read what Burton wrote: "I loathe her today, but now I also pity her. I shall make a point of after tonight never seeing her again."

What made this all the more heartbreaking for Lucy was the fact that she was in awe of Burton. She told me so herself on more than one occasion. It was Lucy who, at a Hollywood party (something she rarely attended) with great trepidation, approached Richard and Elizabeth, like a starstruck fan, and asked them about doing her sitcom, a request she never thought they would agree to in a million years. Taylor had just gotten that 69-karat diamond ring from Burton and Lucy even asked Elizabeth if she could try it on. That moment in time was the catalyst for the next season premiere of *Here's Lucy*. It was a very funny episode about Lucy getting Elizabeth's ring stuck on her finger. Burton played a plumber with a penchant for reciting Shakespeare who gets called in, to get the ring off at any cost.

The trio made the cover of *TV Guide* the week the show aired. And according to Lucy, the week of work with the Burtons was terrific and the only fireworks on the set were those generated off camera by Taylor and Burton themselves, who were forever fighting and making up. I don't know what happened between Lucy and Richard Burton, but I do know that Lucy was devastated to be so maligned in print by a fellow performer.

So we stayed home that New Year's Eve and tried to keep Lucy's spirits up by playing games and wearing silly things on our heads that Tom and I bought from Woolworth's. Lucy liked anything from the five and dime, so long as it didn't cost much more than that. Naturally, backgammon was the game of choice but Lucy taught us a new card game called Pig that Dean Martin had recently taught her. I don't remember much about the game except that you needed lots of dollar bills and you couldn't lose a lot of money—two more things Lucy liked. I was shocked when Lucy, albeit begrudgingly, let me open a bottle of Cristal champagne that Carol Burnett had sent her for Christmas. I toasted Lucy on how blessed we were to have her in our lives, and then we raised our plastic champagne flutes (Lucy would not let us use real ones.) to a happy and healthy 1989.

On New Year's Day Tom and I returned to New York and as usual Lucy was very sorry to see us go. She had nothing to do except go back to Beverly Hills to play backgammon, autograph pictures, turn down television guest spots, and read bad scripts that came her way. After Desi died, Lucy "inherited" lots of stuff from his home in Del Mar, California—old photos, letters, and other memorabilia that was now laying around her house along with tons of her personal mementos. So before I left California I suggested to Lucy that she update her scrapbooks.

Lucy kept scrapbooks from her earliest days as a model in New York and continued to keep them from the time she came to Hollywood as a Goldwyn Girl in 1933. But she fell behind and I knew updating her books would give her something to do, and like anything Lucy started, Lucy finished. So the first couple of months in 1989 were heavily devoted to, as Lucy put it, "Getting my life in order." As it turned out, it would be a prophetic choice of words.

In February 1989, I was doing freelance advertising writing, and I got asked to do two television commercials. One was for Shirley MacLaine's recently published book, *Going Within*, about transforming one's inner self, and the other was for Elizabeth Taylor's new fragrance, Passion, which in stark contrast was strictly about transforming one's outer self. Both commercials were to be shot in Los Angeles, and I would be out there for three weeks. I was very happy to have the chance to see Lucy again so soon. I was scheduled to stay at the Four Seasons Hotel. Lucy offered me the guesthouse. No, she ordered me. "Lucy, I'm coming out to work, not to play backgammon," I warned her.

"We'll see, baby, we'll see."

I met Shirley MacLaine for the first time at her apartment on the day I was hired for the commercial. Long a big fan of hers, I was very excited and nervous about working with her. I was told she had very definite ideas about how she wanted to present this book to the public and that I should just listen and do whatever she told me to do. "Yessing" people to death was not my strong suit, except to Lucy, and I learned that the hard way, so I knew if I had to I could do it with Shirley.

I met Shirley at her apartment on East Fifty-second Street. I was early. Shirley was late—stuck in traffic—and not in a great mood when she arrived. I kept saying to myself, "Think Lucy, think Lucy, and you'll be fine." Shirley greeted me, looked me straight in the eye, and shook my hand with a firm grip, just the way Lucy did the first time I met her. As a matter of fact, there was so much about Shirley that instantly reminded me of Lucy that, after being with her for only a few minutes, I felt as if I had known her for years.

Shirley's concept for advertising the book on television was a simple one; a thirty-second commercial shot in her Malibu home with the glorious Pacific Ocean as the backdrop. Shirley would be talking to someone off camera about the process of "Going Within" so you could find out who you *really* are, thus finding bliss and serenity. "What do you want me to do?" I asked sheepishly.

"You'll be the one I'm talking to," Shirley answered like I was asking the silliest question in the world. She was *very* Lucy. "Now, I'll write the questions that you'll ask me off camera, off microphone. Is that okay with you?"

"Yes, Shirley."

"We'll shoot in Malibu within the next two weeks because that's what's convenient for me."

"Yes, Shirley."

"And I need a date to go to the theatre with me tonight."

"Yes, Shirley," I said automatically not even realizing what she had just asked me.

"Good," she said. "Call up the Shubert Organization, and get two tickets to *Shirley Valentine*, tell them it's for me" (No, Shirley, I'll tell them it's for *me*, I thought) "and then make a reservation for four at Orso after the show."

"Yes, Shirley." I had the "Yes, Shirley" mantra down pat. It was just like being with Lucy. This was going to be a breeze.

Shirley's editor and agent left shortly after our ten-minute meeting and we were alone in her Beekman Place duplex penthouse. She was reading the mail and I was contemplating what to say next. And then it hit me. I'll talk about Lucy. Lucy was a huge fan of Shirley's and vice versa, even though they had rarely seen each other since Lucy did a Shirley MacLaine television special in 1976.

The show was called *Gypsy in My Soul* and it was a tribute to the dancers, the Broadway "Gypsies" as they were known, because they went around like gypsies dancing from one show to the next. (Shirley herself had started out as a gypsy before her big break in *Pajama Game*, when the star Carol Haney broke her ankle and Shirley went on in her place.)

Hot on the heels of the Broadway smash *A Chorus Line*, which was also about dancers in the chorus, *Gypsy in My Soul* had music by Cy Coleman and lyrics by Fred Ebb and was choreographed and directed by Tony Charmoli. The real stars of the show were the dancers who worked their asses off doing some incredible numbers with Shirley. Lucy was as always billed as the "Special Guest Star."

The show was taped over a two-day period—with an audience on the first day for the gypsies' dance numbers and Shirley's solos, and without an audience on the second day for Lucy's numbers. In 1976, having been with Lucy less than a handful of times when Gary' sister, Helen, invited me to the taping, I was too shy to ask Lucy why she wanted to do a show without an audience. I always thought audience reaction was the adrenaline that drove Lucy's talent. I found out later, from Lucy herself, that she was literally scared stiff to dance in front of people—always unsure about her talent, especially since she broke her leg skiing in Snowmass.

The show was a huge success but the taping itself had not gone well at all. There were endless takes of Lucy's song and dance numbers with Shirley and the Gypsies, especially routines where Lucy was so unsteady on her feet that she practically fractured Shirley's shoulder constantly grabbing on to it for support. When Shirley was a few minutes late from the lunch break, a very agitated Lucy flew into a rage, which pissed Shirley off and they both walked off the set to cool off for a while.

I was surprised, to say the least, by Lucy and Shirley's behavior and I wondered if some of those stories I had heard about Lucy's temperamental nature on the set of her series were true. Now I understood why Lucy didn't want an audience of anyone other than Gary, Helen, and me.

After Shirley returned a few phone calls I told her about my close relationship with Lucy especially in the last ten years. I broke her up with my *Terms of Endearment* anecdote about taking Lucy to the movies and her talking all the way through it. And she listened intently when I told her how depressed Lucy had been the last couple of years and how she seldom went out of her house in Beverly Hills.

"Shirley," I said, "if I got Lucy on the phone right now, would you speak to her?" Shirley cheered.

I dialed and when Lucy answered the phone I knew she wasn't in a good mood. "Lucy, it's me. Listen, I'm with some-body who is just dying to talk with you." Lucy told me she just got back from the dentist and had emergency root canal. "So you're in a little pain," I said. "All right, so you're in a lot of pain. All you have to do is listen and nod your head. You don't even have to speak. No, I'm serious! This person is very perceptive, she'll *see* you nod your head, she can do that, really!" Shirley was laughing and jumping up and down. "Lucy, here she is," and with that Shirley grabbed the phone.

"Lucy, what the hell's the matter with your mouth? You know who this is? The last time we were together you prac-tically broke my shoulder, and your legs looked better than mine." Lucy knew who it was and Shirley started crying. "So tell me, Luce, is this kid here with me as nice as he seems?" Shirley paused. "You sure? Because I got a date with him tonight." (I wasn't sure I was ready to tell Lucy about Shirley and me going out together, but it was too late.) Then, after a few seconds Shirley looked up at me, winked, and said, "Yeah, I think he's terrific, too." They spoke for another few minutes about nothing in particular and Shirley made Lucy promise that they would get together when Lucy was in New York or when Shirley was on the coast.

Shirley put me back on the phone. "Where the hell are you going with her tonight?"

"Thanks," I said. "I love you, too, Lucy." And I hung up.

Shirley Valentine was a play about what happens when a lower-middle-class British housewife, on a whim, leaves a note for her husband and decides to get away from her humdrum life and marriage and takes a vacation to Greece. It was terrific. Shirley and I went backstage after the show to congratulate its star, Pauline Collins. Coincidentally, Carole Cook was there, who was one of Lucy's first students when Lucy created the Desilu workshop back in the late 1950s. When Lucy married Gary, Carole tried to remain friends with her, but as he did with so many other of Lucy's pals from when she was married to Desi, Gary dissuaded Lucy from seeing a lot of Carole and they subsequently grew apart.

After we left the theatre, Shirley and I walked over to Orso, a restaurant on West Forty-sixth Street's "Restaurant Row." I had no idea why I had made a reservation for four until I saw Shirley's good buddy Bella Abzug with a very young and handsome male companion sitting at the table waiting for us. We took our seats and Shirley introduced me as her new friend. I liked that. Shirley was a good friend and big political supporter of Bella Abzug, especially during Bella's unsuccessful primary election run for mayor of New York City. Bella and Shirley talked a lot that night and ate very little. I did just the opposite.

We left the restaurant shortly after midnight and Shirley and I decided to walk back to her apartment overlooking the East River, which was about a mile from the restaurant. It was unusually warm for the middle of February and it felt great strolling through the streets with Shirley on my arm. I felt very comfortable in her presence as if I knew her for a long time. Shirley thought that maybe we were friends in a previous life. I just thought that spending so much time with Lucy over the last ten years made it easier for me to be in the company of someone celebrated.

I asked Shirley a lot about the films she had made and the shows she had done on Broadway. I suppose I should have been asking about the books she wrote but as far as I was concerned, I was with a movie star, not an author.

Shirley kept changing the subject—she wanted to talk about Lucy. And I told her something that I had never told anybody. I said that I knew Lucy was going to die very soon and there was nothing I could do about it. I told her that it was more than just a feeling, I was certain of it. I told Shirley how depressed Lucy was—clinically depressed, I was sure. And how Lucy hated the way she looked especially since the stroke, and how she really didn't think anybody cared about her anymore and without work she had no identity, and on and on.

Why don't you suggest psychotherapy to Lucy?" Shirley asked.

"Lucy would never see a psychiatrist, or a 'physiaciatrist,' as Desi would say," I said. Shirley laughed.

We walked in silence and then Shirley asked, "Are you sure she doesn't want to live anymore?"

"Positive," I answered.

"Then, Lee, you have to be with her as much as you can for as long as you can," she said, hugging me tight. I told her that's just what I intended to do.

I flew to Los Angeles on February 27, Elizabeth Taylor's birthday, to shoot the Passion commercial. Chen Sam, Elizabeth's longtime publicist, was planning a small cocktail party in her honor to which I was invited, which Lucy was not at all happy about. "First night here and you're already going out," Lucy scolded.

"Tough choice," I said. "Elizabeth Taylor or Lucille Ball, but Liz wins out," I teased.

"Just get your ass home early," Lucy snapped, "and I want to hear *everything!*"

There was a great deal of hype attached to the Passion launch; Elizabeth made personal appearances in department stores across the country, which drew tens of thousands of people who waited in line for hours for a bottle of perfume and an autographed picture. Elizabeth was notoriously late, but nobody seemed to mind.

Taylor's tardiness was nothing compared to how long she kept everybody waiting on the set when we shot the commercial. If the call time was eight in the morning Elizabeth would show up at one in the afternoon and be ready to shoot at four. That is if she wasn't in spasm from her chronic back condition. But when Elizabeth finally came onto the set each day she looked breathtakingly beautiful and years younger than fifty-seven. A commercial that was scheduled for two days of shooting took over a week to wrap.

Every night when I got back to the house, Lucy demanded a full report on Elizabeth's behavior. I remember one night Lucy and Gary were entertaining Art and Pat Modell. Art Modell at the time owned the Cleveland Browns. When I walked into the dining room during dinner, Lucy stopped Art in mid-sentence and demanded to hear all about Elizabeth's shenanigans on the set that day. As well as what she wore, how long she kept people waiting, and what presents she received. You see, Elizabeth loved receiving gifts so at the beginning of the shoot we were told by Chen Sam that Elizabeth would expect to receive something from someone on the crew or creative team each day we filmed. These gifts were not to be insignificant, so the cost was built in to the commercial's budget. Even Elizabeth's dog, which rarely left her side, was gifted. Lucy had suggested I give Elizabeth a book on etiquette. I chose to give her a cashmere scarf instead.

The day after we completed the Passion commercial I began work on *Going Within* with Shirley. Her house was not what I expected a Malibu beach house to look like. Shirley owned a two-story building that housed a group of apartments. Shirley's was the largest and was filled with movie memorabilia, and lots of crystals—not Waterford, but the kind used for spiritual healing. It was furnished a lot like Lucy's Beverly Hills home. There were green and brown shag rugs, club chairs and ottomans, oversize divans, and lots of Formica countertops.

Shirley was not at all like Elizabeth. She kept everyone waiting only two hours while she first meditated and then fought with her assistant. But once she was on the set, her living room, she knew exactly what she wanted, called all the shots (literally and figuratively), and we wrapped the commercial by the end of the day. Shirley wanted to take Lucy and me out for dinner that evening, at the beach. I really wanted to but I told Shirley that there was no point in asking Lucy. She wouldn't go. And I didn't think I should go without her. Shirley understood completely.

When I got back to the house after the commercial, the backgammon and dinner tables were set. We had one of our favorite meals—veal with vermicelli and a Waldorf salad with miniature marshmallows on top. "It's a celebration meal," Lucy said.

"What are we celebrating, Auntie Mame?"

"That you're mine, again."

Lucie Arnaz had just finished putting together her first night-club act, and was asked to premiere it at MGM Film Center as a fund-raiser for Valley Presbyterian Hospital Center. The benefit was scheduled for March 11, 1989, the day before I was going back to New York. When I arrived in Beverly Hills almost two weeks earlier I suggested to Lucy that she buy a table for the dinner and Lucie's show. "Jeeesus, What the hell do we want to go there for?" Lucy predictably responded even though she knew that I knew she would acquiesce.

Lucy invited an eclectic bunch to the dinner and show: Audrey Meadows, talent manager Ray Katz, Wanda Clark and her husband, Peter, Lucy's publicist Tom Watson, writer Jim Brochu and his friend, Steve Schalchlin, Lucy's driver Frank Gorey, Gary' sister, Helen, Paula Stewart, Gary, and me. It was a wonderful night. Little Lucie was terrific and Big Lucy was proud.

The next day I canceled my plane reservation and stayed on. Lucy was in a funk and faced with a dilemma. She was asked and had agreed to be a presenter with Bob Hope at the Academy Awards on March 27. Now she wanted to back out. "I hate the way I look. My mouth is all crooked. That goddamn wig with all that goddamn netting gives me a goddamn headache, and now take a look at this goddamn script they've sent me," she bitched as she threw it across the backgammon table.

Lucy got upset because she had never heard of any of the nominees and she was afraid she wouldn't be able to see the TelePrompter so she would mispronounce all their names. The truth was she never wanted to do the show in the first place, but Bob called and convinced her that they would look great together. "Goddamn Hope, nobody cares what the hell he looks like but everybody cares what I look like—God, I'm so tired of myself."

I suggested she not wear the wig. "Do your own hair like

you do everyday at home." She looked at me like I had lost my mind. Eventually she calmed down, and I helped her learn the nominee's names, and she went to the Oscars.

Ret Turner designed a fantastic dress for Lucy. A black sheath evening gown with glorious beading and sequins and a slit up the left leg that exposed a showgirl-looking gam practically to the thigh. Lucy and Bob walked on stage to the theme song from I *Love Lucy* and she had the gait of a thoroughbred racehorse. She was a champion. And she was right—nobody cared what Bob Hope looked like. All eyes were on Lucy. She looked sensational and she *knew* it! The Shrine Auditorium audience stood as one for a long and tumultuous ovation. Lucy joked with Bob, mangled some of the nominee's names, and reveled in the spotlight and the applause.

I watched the show alone on Roxbury Drive. "Wait up for me, I'll be home right after I make a fool of myself," Lucy said as she and Gary drove off, dressed to the nines at five in the afternoon. But after the awards were over Lucy reluctantly agreed to go to Spago where legendary agent and raconteur Swifty Lazar threw his annual post–Academy Award bash. Lucy needed one last hurrah at Hollywood. She came home around midnight. Gary said that everybody came by Lucy's table to pay homage. Lucy said, "Jesus, what a bore." That's what Lucy always said after she came home from any party. I knew she didn't mean it that night. But that was Lucy.

I said good night and went to the guesthouse. Lucy immediately buzzed me on the intercom and told me to come back into the house. She was going to get out of the dress and the wig and the makeup and come back downstairs. She wasn't tired and wanted to play backgammon. I wasn't surprised.

In about fifteen minutes Lucy walked into the lanai in her

white bathrobe with the big pink embroidered Lucy. Her hair was in rollers, her frayed pink bunny slippers were on her feet, and at one in the morning, I don't know why, she was carrying her white pocketbook with her backgammon dollars. Her transformation from Miss Lucille Ball to Mrs. Gary Morton was eerie. I could not resist. "Are there two Lucys?" I asked. She looked at me quizzically. "Are you the same Lucy I saw decked out in sequins at the Shrine Auditorium? Or was that a 'Stepford Lucy'?"

We played backgammon for about an hour. Lucy was very unfocused. God only knows what she was thinking. In the middle of a move she just stopped playing, said good night, and went upstairs to bed. I sat at the table for a while rolling the dice and wondering how much more time we would have together.

I woke up early the next morning to meet Thelma at the Beverly Hills Hotel for breakfast. I noticed about a dozen leather scrapbooks on the floor in the living room, with Lucy's name inscribed on the front of each of them. The books were dated with years that spanned from 1933 to 1989. These were the books that Lucy was so busily putting together since the beginning of the year. I tiptoed around them, not wanting to open any until I got Lucy's permission.

"That's my life down there, baby, and nobody really cares." I was startled to see Lucy standing right behind me pointing to the books. She was fully dressed. Her hair was done and her face made up, and she had her white handbag in hand. "That's all of it kid, and do you think anybody will ever look at it?" I went over and opened a book at random. That morning, Thelma would have to eat alone. I grabbed a bialy and cream cheese and a cup of coffee from the kitchen and made myself comfortable on the living room floor.

It *was* Lucy's life, from way back when. There were movie reviews and press clippings from all the B movies she made in the thirties and forties. There were programs from stage shows she did on the road. There was original art from the Broadway production of *Wildcat*. There were matchbook covers from Ciros. There were menus from the Brown Derby. There was a napkin from the Mocambo with a forty-year-old Lucy lipstick print.

But the best part was all the stuff about Lucy and Desi. There were apology notes from Desi while they were dating, begging Lucy for her forgiveness for seeing other women. There were letters from Lucy forgiving him and saying how lonely and lost she was whenever he wasn't around. There was a telegram from Desi to Lucy's mother, DeDe, on the day they eloped in Connecticut telling her how much he loved her daughter, and how he would love her to the day he died. There was the invitation to the Catholic Church wedding they had nine years after their civil ceremony, just to please Desi's mom. There were tons of transcripts from Lucy interviews and hundreds of pictures of the Arnaz's at home and on trips around the world. It took days to get through the books and I made sure I saw everything there was to see.

On Thursday afternoon I told Lucy that on that Sunday night, April 2, I was taking the red-eye back to New York. She pretended not to hear me. That morning Gary left for a golf tournament but he would be home Monday morning and I had to get back to Tom and to my work. "Did you hear what I said Lucy? I'm leaving Sunday night right after *60 Minutes*."

"Yeah, sure," she said. Lucy loved to watch *60 Minutes*. She was absolutely crazy about Diane Sawyer. Every time Lucy saw her on television she would say, "What a dame, I have to meet her someday."

On Thursday night, I went out to dinner with a very talented singer/actor friend named Jason Graae who came by the house to pick me up and to meet Lucy. Lucy begrudgingly made a reservation for Jason and me at Spago, which at the time was one of the trendiest restaurants in town. With Gary gone and the help off I felt bad leaving Lucy all alone so I begged her to join us. "No way, and I don't know why the hell you want to go there for. It's such a bore!" Lucy said to Jason and me.

"You'll never change, Auntie Mame," I whispered to Lucy as I kissed her good night.

"Bet your ass, my little love," she whispered back.

Before we were allowed to leave the house, Lucy made Jason promise he would drive carefully, an unintentionally funny admonishment from Lucy. "And get home before midnight," she ordered.

"Lucy," I said, "I'm just going to dinner, not my senior prom." Lucy said she would leave the side door unlocked for me. I said, "Nothing doing," so she gave me the key to the bottom lock only.

"I'll leave the top lock open so you just use the bottom one."

As Jason slowly, carefully backed his car out of the driveway while Lucy stood watching his every move in the doorway, I shouted à la Jimmy Durante, "Good night Mrs. Goldaper, whoever you are." Lucy's laugh rocked Roxbury Drive.

We had a blast at Spago. The food was terrific and the service was even better. Doors were opened for us, chairs were pulled back, and napkins were refolded. I decided that night that Lucy should make all my dinner reservations on both coasts. Lucy loved the pizza from Spago, the one with smoked salmon, crème fraiche, chives, red onion and a dollop of caviar, so I asked the headwaiter if the kitchen could prepare a pie for her, which I would take with me. Ten minutes later the pizza came out of the oven, delivered to our table by Wolfgang Puck himself with his compliments. He was less generous with our tab. Pizza for two was one hundred and twenty-five dollars.

It was a very hot and unusually sticky evening when we left the restaurant and drove back to Lucy's. In fact the last few weeks the weather in Los Angeles had been more like the middle of summer than early spring. I even managed to get a deep tan despite the little time I was allowed to spend in the exercise yard of "Paradise Prison." It was nearly midnight when Jason dropped Lucy's pizza and me off at the house. I flashed the single key Lucy gave me to Jason and he drove off. It was very still and very dark and I realized it was the first time I had ever been outside at night alone on the streets of Beverly Hills.

I put the key in the lock, turned the tumbler, heard the lock open and yet I could not get in the house. I took the key out, stuck it back in, relocked the lock, tried opening it again and still the door would not open. Someone had locked the top lock. I started talking to myself, out loud.

"Okay," I said, "Don't panic, go to a corner phone and call the house." "There are no corner phones in Beverly Hills." I answered back. "Okay, then what would Lucy Ricardo do in this situation?" I started laughing. "She would go around to the side of the house, climb over the wall, and go into the guesthouse, which was always unlocked." "But the wall is taller than the one Lucy climbed over to get into Richard Widmark's house and besides I don't have Ethel to give me a boost." "I know, I'll throw some pebbles at Lucy's window like she did when she and Ethel were locked on their brown-

stone roof and needed to attract their neighbor's attention."
So I threw pebbles and all I managed to do was attract the
attention of every poodle and cocker spaniel guard dog on
Roxbury Drive. When the barking subsided I tried calling out,
"Lucy, Lucy, Lucy." And then Lucy's bedroom light went out.
I was fresh out of ideas and Lucy episodes.

I was hot and tired of carrying around Lucy's pizza pie and I
had to pee very badly. I knew that taking a walk at night in Beverly Hills was a misdemeanor. I wondered if taking a leak
would be considered a felony. I didn't have time to find out. I
relieved myself right there on Lucy's front lawn. How many
fans can say that? I picked up my Spago designer pizza box and
decided to walk to the Beverly Hills Hotel, which was about a
half-mile away so I could use the phone to call the house and
wake Lucy from a sound sleep. She'd really like that.

About twenty yards into my journey I was stopped dead in
my tracks by the whirl of a spinning police light and the
sound of a siren that was so quiet it wouldn't even wake Lucy
up. It was a Beverly Hills patrol car—from a police department
so chic it has an unlisted phone number, so they say. "Can I
help you?" asked the polite policeman in a very nonthreaten-
ing tone.

"Well, you won't believe this officer, sir, but I'm a guest
of Lucille Ball," pointing toward the house (like they didn't
know where she lived) "and my friend just dropped me off.
You see my friend and I had dinner at Spago" (now pointing
to my Spago pizza box) "and I got locked out because someone locked the top lock by mistake and I only have the key
to the bottom." I stopped my story there because I could see
from the expression on the officer's face that he didn't believe
a word I was saying, and neither did I. And I was there.

The next thing I knew they invited me into the squad car,

the backseat, while the officer gets back in the driver's seat and he and his buddy cop next to him escort me to the Beverly Hills Hotel so I could use the phone. About five minutes later I got out of the patrol car and was accompanied through the lobby by both officers, who insisted on going with me to the phone to call Lucy. It was lovely walking past the Polo Lounge with a cop on either side of you.

I knew I would wake Lucy up but I figured she of all people would find this whole thing funny—just like one big Lucy episode. I did wake her and I jokingly said that I was in police custody at the Beverly Hills Hotel. The joke backfired—neither she nor the policemen thought it was funny. One cop grabbed the phone to talk with Lucy, who was stuttering so badly, he hardly understood a word she said. I got back on the phone and reassured her that everything was fine and told her what had happened and that I was coming home.

I told the cops I would take a cab but they insisted on driving me back to the house. They could not have been nicer to me on the ride back and I was sure that they wanted to meet Lucy in person. And they did. At one-thirty in the morning Lucy stood at the side door, half asleep with her hair in curlers signing autographs for the cops, their wives, their kids, and for practically the whole Beverly Hills Police Department. By the time they pulled out of her driveway fifteen minutes later, Lucy was wide awake and in great spirits. So as long as Lucy was up we shared a pizza and played a few games of backgammon.

The next morning the mystery of the locked door was solved. Chris and Roza, the couple who now worked at the house (Kim and Choo had retired) thought that I was home and had double-locked the door when they arrived home the night before. I ate breakfast at the house thinking it was best to stay away from the Beverly Hills Hotel for a day or so. By the afternoon everybody Lucy spoke to knew what happened to me on the way home from Spago. With her penchant for embellishing stories, by the time she finished telling everyone about the incident, I was arrested for peeing on her front lawn, accused of stealing a pizza from Spago, and handcuffed to the front door of the Polo Lounge while being frisked by four cops.

After the Spago incident, I knew my parole would be revoked and I would not be allowed to leave the house at all for the rest of the weekend. Not until the limousine picked me up at nine o'clock Sunday night for the red-eye back to New York. I couldn't care less. I wanted to spend as much time with Lucy as I possibly could. We played lots of back-gammon, just the two of us. Gary was away and Chris and Roza had left on their vacation so there was nobody home except Lucy and me. It was a very special weekend. But I had no idea it would be our last one together.

On Saturday afternoon right in the middle of a backgam-mon game, Lucy stopped playing and asked me if I was all right. I told her I was fine, and then she said, "I mean, baby, are you *really* all right?"

I thought I knew what she was getting at but I still wasn't sure. "What do you mean, Lucy?" I asked seriously.

"Well, you know, do you have that, you know that, that thing that's going around?" Lucy said stammering.

"You mean, AIDS?" I asked incredulously, not because it wasn't a legitimate question to ask in 1989, but because Lucy could not bring herself to say the word AIDS out loud. "No, Lucy," I said, "of course I don't have AIDS."

"Well, Swen Swenson has it and I don't want you to go to his house with Paula Stewart when you're back in New York,"

Lucy warned. (Swen Swenson was a very talented singer and dancer who appeared with Lucy in *Wildcat* and who was nominated for a Tony Award in 1963 for Best Featured Actor in a Musical for his performance in *Little Me*. He died of AIDS in the early nineties.)

"Why wouldn't you want me to go to his house?" I asked.

"Because you can't eat with the same knives and forks as he does," Lucy said.

"Lucy, you know that's not true. What are you talking about? You can't get AIDS from somebody's silverware. What's the matter with you?" I was clearly upset and I was getting her upset just talking about AIDS, so I dropped the subject and we continued playing backgammon. A few minutes later she started really sobbing.

"Promise me you won't go. I couldn't bear to have something happen to you." As usual, Lucy had the last word, and I promised I wouldn't visit Swen. It was very sad and more than a bit frightening that a woman as bright as Lucy was still in the dark about AIDS in April, 1989.

Earlier in the week Lucy received a note from her next-door neighbor, an industrialist originally from the Midwest, who had bought Jack Benny's home. He and his wife were giving a rather large tent party that Saturday evening around their pool and they wanted to advise Lucy that there would be a lot of vehicular traffic on Roxbury as well as an unusual amount of noise until around midnight. They apologized for any inconvenience and wanted to let her know well in advance of the day.

The night of the party, after Lucy and I raided the refrigerator for leftovers for dinner and were playing backgammon in the lanai, Lucy suddenly got very curious about the folks next door and their Saturday night soirée. "I have an idea," she said. I had never heard real-life Lucy utter those immortal

Lucy Ricardo words, but when she said them there was such a twinkle in those baby blues of hers that I knew she had some clever ruse up her sleeve, and I couldn't wait to find out what it was.

I followed her through the house out the side door and into the narrow alleyway that separated Lucy's and her neighbor's home. "I'm just dying to find out what the tent looks like and who's there," Lucy whispered. She looked around and spotted some milk crates in the corner. "Baby, bring those over and we'll climb on top of them and see what's going on next door." She called me baby but she might as well have called me, "Ethel," that's how much I felt like her second banana. And the next thing I know Lucille Ball and her faithful sidekick are peeping through the trellis and palm fronds checking out their neighbors' pool party.

Lucy was fascinated by the goings-on, commenting on everything, and eyeing everybody who ironically would have given their eyeteeth to meet the crazy redhead on the other side of the wall. After a half-hour or so Lucy lost interest and we went back to backgammon. But while it lasted it was such great fun to see Lucy joyful again!

We quit playing well after midnight long after the party next door ended and Roxbury Drive was once again still. I was in the guesthouse talking to Tom in New York when Lucy buzzed me on the intercom. "Come upstairs to my bedroom, right away, I need you." I immediately thought of Gloria Swanson as Norma Desmond in *Sunset Boulevard*, summoning William Holden, the young writer, to her boudoir. I asked Lucy if she was feeling all right. She said there was nothing wrong with her but there was something wrong with her television set and I would have to fix it. I told Lucy I would be up right away and then I told Tom that I couldn't talk to him anymore because Madam had sent for me. We both laughed when I said that if he didn't hear from me by the next morning that I might be floating facedown in Lucy's swimming pool just like poor Bill Holden at the beginning of the classic film.

I walked through the garden in my shorts and T-shirt, and I chuckled when I saw my reflection at the deep end of the pool. I entered the house through the sliding glass doors of the lanai and climbed the stairs to Lucy's bedroom. I had rarely gone up there. The last time was almost a year earlier when Lucy had the stroke and I brought her all that lilac from New York.

This really was like *Sunset Boulevard*, except I was a gay Bill Holden. Now, how's that for an oxymoron. All of a sudden, I got nervous—I don't know why—and started sweating. I knocked on Lucy's door. "It's open. Just come on in." I walked in and Lucy was propped up in her bed surrounded by umpteen pink and lavender pillows, with her toy poodle, Tinker, sound asleep at her side. A babushka was tied around Lucy's head and she had mounds of cold cream on her face. A reading light, which was on next to her bed, was the room's only illumination. She was staring at a television with no picture or sound. For some reason I was afraid to be with Lucy. "What's wrong?" Lucy asked.

I jumped. "Do I look like something's wrong?"

"I mean with the TV," she said. "Here," Lucy continued, "take the remote and see what you can do. I was playing with it and maybe I screwed it up." I went to her side of the bed and yanked it out of her hand. After madly pushing every button on the remote control, the picture and sound finally came back. Lucy faintly smiled and I just wanted to get out as fast as I could. "Thanks for taking such good care of me dear, and call me when you get back to the guesthouse."

There was no need to. The intercom was buzzing like crazy when I opened my door. "What took you so long?" Lucy said and then hung up.

On Sunday morning I packed my bags and took an early morning dip in the pool. As I was drying off I noticed Lucy walking across the garden toward the pool house. It was not even ten o'clock but Lucy was fully dressed and made up. She looked absolutely beautiful. She was wearing a blue and white striped man-tailored shirt, white slacks, white sandals, and she carried her signature white lunchbox with the baggie full of one-dollar bills. It was a sunny, windy day and her hair that was freshly combed out was gently billowing in the breeze. She seemed almost angelic walking toward me in what looked like slow motion. To this day, it's the image of Lucy I conjure up when ever I think of her. On that day I remember thinking to myself, "She looks like she's in heaven already."

We played backgammon in the pool house all Sunday afternoon. It was our favorite place to play. At five o'clock, out of the blue, Lucy said she wanted to show me a video. She said she wasn't sure how to use the VCR so I quickly told her I would take care of it. I didn't want a repeat of what happened the night before. We strolled together, arm and arm, in the late-day sun through the garden back into the house and into Gary's den. Lucy pulled down *Carol plus Two*, Carol Burnett's first television special from the 1960s, which guest-starred Zero Mostel and Lucy. I had only seen it once and I was curious as to why she wanted me to see it again now. "I just want you to watch this one sketch with me. It's my favorite and Carol is so funny. God, is she good!" Lucy adored Carol Burnett and always raved about her work. The feeling was mutual. Carol was crazy about Lucy. They appeared on each other's shows and Carol always said the most wonderful things about Lucy, giving Lucy's comedic influence on her much of the credit for her own success.

When Lucy told me to fast-forward to the "Good-bye, Baby" skit I was surprised because I knew Lucy was in it and Lucy did not like to watch herself on television. Occasionally when I was in the den watching an I *Love Lucy* tape, she would sneak up behind me, but when I saw she was there she would invariably leave the room.

The sketch featured Carol and Lucy as sisters. Lucy, on her way to the airport to go on her first vacation in twenty years, visits Carol who has a new baby. Carol wants the baby to say, "Good-bye," to Lucy, and tells Lucy that if she says "Good-bye baby," the baby will say it back. Lucy lovingly obliges and says "Good-bye baby." Nothing happens. Lucy tries again, but nothing happens. She tries a few antics but no "Good-bye."

Lucy kisses Carol and tells her sister that she has a great kid, and she's sure that someday soon her baby will say "Good-bye," to someone, but just not to her and not today. Nothing doing. Against her will Carol holds Lucy there until her baby says, "Good-bye." Lucy keeps shouting, "Good-bye, baby" until she can no longer stand it, and then she begins screaming into the baby carriage, "Good-bye, baby! Good-bye, baby!! Good-bye, baby!!! Did you hear what I said? Are you deaf or something?" And on and on. Lucy finally has to bribe the baby with five hundred dollars and a trip to Miami before the baby goo-goos a good-bye.

Lucy and I watched the sketch three times and we laughed till it hurt. Then Lucy cooked us franks and beans, a recipe that after nine years she nearly perfected, although she still overcooked the beans, and we ate dinner on stack tables in the den while we watched Diane Sawyer on *60 Minutes*. It was the best afternoon I had ever spent with Lucy.

After *60 Minutes* we played backgammon until the limousine driver rang the bell. Then Lucy started to cry. I grabbed my bags as Lucy grabbed my arm and we walked down the hall. "Remember," I said, "No tears and no good-byes, that's what we always said to each other whenever we left one another."

Lucy snapped back, "What do you mean no good-byes. Good-bye, baby." I said nothing. I opened the door and the driver took my bags. Lucy stepped outside in to the night air, and again said, "Good-bye, baby." I checked my pockets pretending to look for something, and paid no attention. Lucy started shouting "Good-bye, baby!" I started talking to the driver, completely ignoring her. The driver didn't know what to do. Lucy started screaming at the top of her lungs, "Good-bye, baby! Good-bye, baby! Good-bye, baby! What are you deaf or something?"

Finally, the driver turned to me and said, "I think the lady is talking to you."

I said, "Let's go."

I got in the car and we slowly pulled out of the driveway with Lucy, now at the curb still screaming "Good-bye, baby! Good-bye, baby! Good-bye, baby!" I lowered the window, stuck my hand out the window, held it high, and waved back. As we rode off the limousine driver asked if Miss Ball always acted like that. I was too choked up to answer.

When I got back to New York I called Lucy every day. She was very depressed and nothing I said made her laugh. In May she was supposed to come east to receive an honorary degree from Jamestown Community College and then go to Buffalo where the Shea Theatre chain was presenting her with the first annual Lucille Ball Award for outstanding people from the western New York area. "This is what happens when you can't work anymore. They give you degrees and awards," she groused. "Baby, I can't, I won't go without you," she said.

"I'll be there, you know I will," I said holding back tears. Neither of us ever got to go.

On April 17, Lucy was rushed to Cedars-Sinai in Los Angeles with a ruptured aorta. She endured nine hours of surgery and was recovering well. Ironically Fritz Friedman's partner Dr. Jeffrey Krebs was on duty when Lucy was rushed to the hospital, and he became one of her attending physicians. Each day, Jeffrey gave us practically hourly updates on Lucy's condition. He even relayed messages from me to Lucy because no phone calls were permitted.

On April 25, Lucy was progressing so well that Jeffrey said she would be moving into a private suite the next day. Gary called that night to tell us the only way to reach Lucy would be to tell the operator you were calling for Diane Belmont. Diane Belmont was Lucy's nom de plume for a short time in New York when she was modeling for Hattie Carnegie. She called herself Diane Belmont because when she was a kid, Lucy always loved the name Diane and she chose the last name when she and a bunch of pals were riding on Long Island past Belmont Racetrack. Gary said Lucy was expecting my call the next morning. I couldn't wait.

On the morning of April 26, I was at the advertising agency when I received a call from Judy Gibson. Judy and her husband Bob Van Pelt were good friends of ours and were the godparents of Lucie and Larry's first child, Simon. They were living out in Los Angeles at the time so I was surprised to hear Judy's voice when I picked up the phone at nine-thirty in the morning New York time. "Hey girl, what are you doing up so early in the morning?" I said. For a moment there was silence and then she started sobbing and I knew. "Judy, what's wrong? Tell me, what's wrong?" I started crying, too. "Is it Lucy?"

Lucy had awoken about five in the morning with a pain in her lower back. A few minutes later she lost consciousness and died. Was Lucy alone in her room when the fatal attack occurred? Her daughter Lucie recalls being told that her mother rang for a nurse when the pain began. I have often wondered how frightened she must have been. A few hours earlier TrudyArcudiPrivateDuty had gone back to her home in the Valley to get some much needed rest and was not with Lucy when she passed away. The death certificate listed a ruptured aorta. I think Lucy died because she simply did not want to live anymore.

The Season Finale

I HUNG UP THE PHONE WITH JUDY and I began shaking uncontrollably. I looked at the clock on my desk, the one that Lucy had given me for Christmas the year before. It said nine thirty-five. Lucy was dead for a little more than an hour. I called Tom and when he picked up the phone I started to cry, "Lucy's gone, I'm coming home." He started to weep and I hung up the phone and jumped in a taxi. Immediately I heard a news bulletin come on the radio: "Lucille Ball, one of the world's most beloved entertainers, died at Cedars-Sinai Hospital in Los Angeles at five-twenty this morning. She was seventy-seven years old."

When I got home the phone never stopped ringing. The answering machine took all the calls. I flopped down in a cold sweat on our couch in the den. The phone rang again and this time Tom answered it. I told him that I didn't want to talk to anybody except my mother. My father was having open-heart surgery that morning and I knew my mother would want to speak with me when the operation was over. Tom answered and said I wasn't available and asked who was calling. "Hold on, I'll put him on. Lee, it's for you." I just shook my head no. Tom cupped his hand over the receiver and said, "Lee, it's Shirley MacLaine."

"Lee, honey, I'm so sorry." Shirley's voice broke on the phone. "I'm in Seattle shooting a film and I just heard the news." She gave me her phone number on the set and said to please call if I needed to talk. Then we both started to cry.

Later that afternoon, Tom and I took a walk in Central Park. It was a glorious spring afternoon. The trees were beginning to blossom. The forsythia was in full bloom, and lilac, Lucy's favorite flower, which grew alongside the Sheep Meadow, was starting to bud. We walked for about an hour, saying nothing. We were too numb to speak. We could not believe Lucy was gone.

Mark and Betty Cohen came over early that evening. Lucy's death was the lead story on every newscast, local and national. *Entertainment Tonight* devoted their entire half-hour to her. CBS produced an hour-long special tribute to Lucy at ten o'clock that night, hosted by Walter Cronkite. We watched and we laughed at Lucy the way we had laughed at her for forty years. But it was almost unimaginable that I would never laugh with her again.

The next day Lucy's face graced the front page of every newspaper in the world. The *New York Times* ran a page-one obituary with two additional pages inside, and an editorial entitled "We Love Lucy Too." The following Monday she was on the cover of *People*, *Time*, and *Newsweek*. *The Star*, *The Globe*, and *The Enquirer*, of course, made her passing front-page news, conjuring up the most sensational lurid stories about her final days.

There was no funeral service for Lucy. That is exactly what Lucy wanted. I know because she told me so herself one night in Beverly Hills when the two of us were alone at home watching *A Star Is Born*. After we saw the scene where Judy Garland is mobbed on the way out of the church after attending the funeral for her husband James Mason, Lucy laughed and said, "I will kill Gary if I ever have a funeral like that." The day after she died she was cremated and her ashes were placed in a crypt beside her mother. Gary, Lucie, and Larry were the only ones present at Forest Lawn.

Lucie Arnaz was planning three memorial services for Lucy: in Los Angeles, Chicago, and New York City. Each was to take place on Monday, May 8, at eight o'clock in the evening in their respective time zones. Mondays at eight was when I Love Lucy originally aired when it premiered in 1951.

Lucie called Tom and me and asked if we would organize the service in New York. She wanted us to do it at St. Ignatius Loyola, a Catholic Church on Park Avenue and Eighty-third Street in Manhattan. Lucy was not a Catholic but Lucie and Larry knew the priest and wanted him to preside over the service in the sanctuary. The services would be open to the public on a first-come basis. St. Ignatius held close to two thousand people and we knew the crowd would overflow into the streets. Lucie asked if I had any ideas about who her mother would have wanted to give her eulogy. I immediately thought of Diane Sawyer. "Did she know her?" Lucie asked.

"No," I said, "But she always wanted to meet her."

Diane Sawyer had just left 60 Minutes to go over to ABC, where she and Sam Donaldson were about to start an hour-long newsmagazine called Prime Time Live.

I knew the chances of Diane Sawyer agreeing to deliver Lucy's eulogy were next to none, but I called her office at ABC and left a message. The next day Diane herself called me back and agreed although she admitted she was more than a little surprised. "Are you sure Lucy meant me, and not Diane Keaton?"

The press reported on the upcoming memorial service,

billed as a "Celebration of the Life of Lucille Ball." The crowds lined up at dawn to get a seat inside the church. To accommodate the hundreds of fans who could not get in, there were speakers placed on Park Avenue so people outside the church could hear the service. Tom and I read passages from the Bible. Judy Gibson sang "Make Someone Happy," Lucy's favorite song. Then Diane Sawyer spoke.

Diane's eulogy was appropriately called "Is There Laughter in Heaven?" And she eloquently made the case that if Lucy was indeed in heaven, there was no doubt in her mind that if they weren't laughing *before* Lucy got there they were sure laughing now. Then Diane spoke about how familiar Lucy had become in our collective psyche. "Isn't it funny," Diane said, "I cannot for the life of me remember how the furniture was laid out in the living room of the house I grew up in, but I can remember where every stick of furniture was in the Ricardo house." Two thousand celebrants nodded their heads in agreement.

Lastly, Diane acknowledged her love for Lucy, for a woman she had never met, but felt she knew all her life. Everyone applauded when she finished. Diane left the church immediately after the service and I never had a chance, until many years later, to thank her personally for her beautifully touching words and for what they meant, especially to me.

In addition to the memorial services Lucie also wanted to get friends, family, and Desilu alumni together for a picnic in Lucy's memory and she thought a great day to do that would be on Mother's Day, Sunday May 14. The picnic would be reminiscent of the ones Lucy and Desi gave every year for all their employees and their families.

When Lucie invited us to the picnic, Gary insisted we stay at the guesthouse and we agreed. It was a big mistake. When we arrived at the house Gary was moving furniture around—

taking a television set from the lanai and putting it into his bedroom, moving a plant from the pool house into his den. When I asked him what he was doing he said, "From now on things are gonna be the way I want them in the house. Now it's my home and nobody is going to tell me what to do." I was dumbfounded.

It turned out that the home Gary shared with Lucy for almost thirty years was not his after all. According to the terms of Lucy's trust it was to be sold. Gary stayed on for almost two years after Lucy's death, until the attorneys more or less insisted that he vacate the house. It was put on the market for an exorbitant asking price of close to seven million dollars. It stayed on the market for a couple of years and finally sold for somewhere around three million dollars.

The new owners changed much of the interior and put a whole new façade on 1000 North Roxbury. A couple of years ago I drove by the house with my friend David Zippel—it was the first time I had seen it since Lucy died. The house was virtually unrecognizable from the one I spent so much time in. It mattered little. Cars and tour buses still slowed and stopped in front—no matter who was living there, it would still always belong to Lucy.

As Gary busily rearranged things we brought our bags into the guesthouse. We didn't even unpack. We just looked around and cried. It was inconceivable that Lucy wasn't right there with us barking orders. That night Tom and I went out for dinner. We came back late and hardly slept.

The next morning Gary went out to play golf and Lucie came by the house to see us. She wanted to clean out her mother's bathroom cabinets and she asked me to help. We walked through Lucy's bedroom and into her dressing room and bath. Everything was so still. The emptiness was palpable.

In one of the drawers under the sink was an unmarked and tattered manila envelope with a rubber band tied around it. Lucie grabbed the envelope from the drawer, and when it tore apart dozens of pieces of paper fell to the bathroom floor. They were love letters that Desi and Lucy wrote to each other during the war in the 1940s—when Desi was touring the country for the Army and Navy Relief and Lucy was making movies in Hollywood. Lucy had held onto these letters for nearly fifty years and their contents were even too personal for her scrapbooks. Now Lucie has them and cherishes them as a reminder of her parents' once great love affair.

Lucie and I have gotten much closer since her mother's death. I'm happy about that. We see each other for dinners in Manhattan and for joint birthday celebrations for Tom and her, who were born three days apart in 1951. When we're together she introduces me as her only living relative in the New York Metropolitan area. Occasionally I see Desi Jr. when he comes to Manhattan.

Thelma Orloff, Lucy's pal for over half a century, died from kidney failure in 1993. Gary died of lung cancer in 1999. Gary's sister, Helen, still lives in West Hollywood. Paula Stewart resides in Los Angeles where she still does some interior design, although I hear she has resumed her career in show business. Frank Gorey is retired and lives on the West Coast, although he loves to travel the world. Wanda Clark lives and works in L.A. and although I don't see her very much we keep in touch more than ever via e-mail. She's a terrific lady and I so value her friendship.

I bought Lucy's white Chrysler LeBaron convertible, the one that I used to drive when I was in Palm Springs, from her estate. I shipped the car to our home on Kauai where I drive it to this day. The car still speaks to us: "A door is ajar, buckle your seat belt, your fuel is low." But now the voice sounds more like Lucy.

The picnic was held at the onetime estate of Robert Taylor in Mandeville Canyon in Los Angeles. Fifty people attended, including Gary, Lucie Arnaz, Larry Luckinbill, their children Simon, Joe, and Kate, Larry's ex-wife, Robin Strasser, Desi Arnaz Jr., Audrey Meadows, Mary Wickes, Paula Stewart, TrudyArcudiPrivateDuty, Onna White, Irma Kusely, Frank Gorey, Wanda Clark, Tom Watson, Lucy's writers, Madelyn Pugh and Bob Carroll, Tom Wells and me.

It was supposed to be a day of celebration but for me it was a day without Lucy. We told stories about Lucy and watched *Lucy* reruns and ate all the food Lucy loved to eat like pimento cheese sandwiches, tapioca pudding, and would you believe . . . Spam. All of us tried so hard to make believe we were having fun, but there really wasn't any fun without Lucy. And oh, would she have hated this picnic! "What a bore. Did you ever see so many wax works in your life. Let's get our asses home and play backgammon!" That's what Lucy would have said. That's what I wanted so much to hear.

When the picnic was over we drove back to the house and immediately collected our bags from the guesthouse. We called a car service to take us to the airport so we could catch the red-eye back to New York. Then we sat outside and waited in silence. The car pulled into the driveway and it was the same driver who took me to the airport when I left Lucy's house for the last time in early April. He offered his condolences and I thanked him as he lifted our bags into the trunk. Tom got into the car, but I could not move. I was paralyzed with sadness. Images of Lucy swirled around my brain.

Just then I thought of something I hadn't thought about in

a long time. A few years ago, Lucy and I were flying back from Baltimore in a small plane late one night. Earlier that day we had seen Lucie and Larry star in the musical I Do, I Do. When the audience realized that Lucille Ball was in the audience they went wild. Everywhere we went that day—the theater, at the airport, in the restaurant, Lucy was surrounded by adoring fans.

As I sat next to Lucy in the plane, I asked her something I never had before: "Lucy, how do you relate to all your fame?" She leaned back in her seat and said, "I once read an article that said I'm known in ninety-nine percent of the households in America. And I'm looking down at all these lights and I'm thinking that if I rang any one of those doorbells, they would invite me in. And when I first came to New York in the late twenties nobody knew who I was, and nobody invited me in, and I had to save my nickels for tea. And now everybody wants to give me everything for nothing." Then she sighed and closed her eyes. It was the only time Lucy talked to me about being famous.

I finally took a couple of steps toward the car and then I turned back one last time to look at the house. There was Lucy—standing right outside the front door, in a man-tailored blue and white striped shirt, white sandals, a white pocketbook in one hand, a plastic bag with backgammon dollar bills in the other, and her orange hair, freshly coiffed, was blowing in the breeze. She winked at me. I whispered, "Goodbye, baby." She then turned her back, raised her fingers high in the air, and waved. And then she was gone.

Then I turned, got in the car, and went home.

✳ *Appendix* ✳

LUCY'S FAVORITES

Everybody loves Lucy. But who and what did Lucy love?

Below is a list compiled from what Lucy herself told me through the years of our friendship. The people and things are in no particular order. And I'm sure the list is by no means complete.

FAVORITE TELEVISION PERSONALITIES

Vivian Vance

Gale Gordon

Carol Burnett

Vanna White

Diane Sawyer

John Ritter

Mark Linn-Baker

Gary Coleman

Roseanne Barr

Oprah Winfrey

Ann Sothern

Appendix

FAVORITE MOVIE STARS
Carole Lombard
Shirley MacLaine
Spencer Tracy
Katharine Hepburn
Audrey Hepburn
William Holden
Liza Minnelli
Gary Cooper
Henry Fonda
Goldie Hawn

FAVORITE MOVIES
Cabaret
Terms of Endearment
My Fair Lady
Funny Girl
A Star Is Born (Garland/Mason version)

FAVORITE SINGERS
Bobby Darrin
Dean Martin
Barbra Streisand
Judy Garland
Perry Como

FAVORITE ENTERTAINERS
Bob Hope
Tommy Tune
Wayne Newton
Flip Wilson
Sammy Davis, Jr.

Bette Midler

Lily Tomlin

Maurice Chevalier

FAVORITE FLOWERS

lilac

yellow roses

red and white carnations

gladiolas

FAVORITE COLORS

mauve

aquamarine

purple

chocolate brown

FAVORITE FOODS

franks and beans

tapioca pudding

Spam

Jell-O with Kraft mayonnaise and a cherry on top

royal beluga caviar

grilled cheese sandwiches

Spaghetti and meatballs

Waldorf salad

   (Canned Mandarin orange sections and diced apples
   mixed with Kraft mayonnaise, topped with pecans and
   miniature marshmallows)

pimento cheese sandwiches

oyster stew

chicken chop suey

raspberries

Appendix

FAVORITE RESTAURANTS

Joe's Pier 52 (New York City)

Mattco's (Westwood, California)

Elaine's (New York City)

Chasen's (Beverly Hills)

Carino (New York City)

The Oyster Bar (New York City)

Patsy's (New York City)

Dominick's (Palm Springs, California)

P. J. Bernstein's Delicatessen (New York City)

FAVORITE *I LOVE LUCY* EPISODES

"Queen of the Gypsies"*

"Vitametavegamin"

"The Chocolate Factory"

"Grape Stomping"

"Lucy and Don Loper"

"The Home Freezer"

"Lucy Meets William Holden"

"Lucy Gives Birth"

"Friends of the Friendless"

*Lucy's all-time favorite

✳ *Index* ✳